The Crisis of Democracy
In the advanced industrial economies

Robert Corfe is not only a prolific writer on political and socio-economic topics, but is experienced in party political life both locally and on the national level. His successful journalistic career dates from the 1960s, and through extensive study, he has acquired considerable knowledge of the social sciences, history and philosophy. After a long business career in senior management in a manufacturing environment, promoting home-based productivity, and later as a management consultant, he founded the Campaign for Industry in 1987 to confront the damaging tendencies of international finance. Lord Gregson of Stockport was elected President of the association, and for over a decade Corfe wrote many pamphlets on the problems of industry and the question of more widely distributing the assets of wealth. His ten years in Scandinavia, in addition to business travels throughout the world, have given him a broad perspective of the needs of all humanity.

By the same author –

Autobiographical –

Death in Riyadh
dark secrets in hidden Arabia

My Conflict with A Soviet Spy
The story of the Ron Evans spy case

The Girl from East Berlin
a romantic docu-drama of the East-West divide

This Was My England
the story of a childhood

Sociological –

Land of The Olympians
papers from the enlightened Far North

Deism and Social Ethics
the role of religion in the third millennium

Islam and The New Totalitarianism
fundamentalism's threat to world civilisation

Populism Against Progress
and the collapse of aspirational values

Political –

The Future of Politics
With the demise of the left/right confrontational system

Social Capitalism in Theory and Practice
(3 volumes)

Egalitarianism of The Free Society
and the end of class conflict

The Democratic Imperative
the reality of power relationships in the nation state

The Death of Socialism
The irrelevance of the traditional left and the call for a progressive politics of universal humanity

The Crisis of Democracy

in the advanced industrial economies

Robert Corfe

Arena Books

Arena Books
6 Southgate Green
Bury St. Edmunds
IP33 2BL.

www.arenabooks.co.uk

Corfe, Robert- 1935
The Crisis of Democracy in the advanced industrial economies

British Library cataloguing in Publication Data. A Catalogue record
for this book is available from the British Library.

ISBN 978-1-911593-30-0

BIC categories:- HPS, KJD, KLG, LNH, JFSC, JHBA, JHBL, JKSB, JF, JFH.

Printed & bound by Lightning Source UK

Cover design
by Jason Anscomb

Typeset in
Times New Roman

PREFACE

"The nation state is still the right level at which to modernise any number of social and fiscal policies and to develop new forms of governance and shared ownership intermediate between public and private ownership which is one of the major challenges for the century ahead."

Thomas Piketty, *Capital in the Twenty-First Century*, Harvard University Press, 2014, p. 573.

Progress has moved ahead at such a pace that it has not been possible for thought to keep abreast in comprehending the nature of change. This is leading to a politically chaotic situation, for the superstitious ideas of outdated ideology are maintained in a world where they no longer have credibility.

The greatest superstition of all is the validity of the left/right struggle in political life in the belief it continues to advance the cause of democracy or the better socio-economic interests of the majority. To most, the idea of political life without the existence of a left/right conflict is unthinkable. It is argued that if one is neither a Conservative nor a left-leaning supporter, then one must necessarily be a centrist, and yet those supporting the centre are in no better position, since they tend to advance the worse or weaker aspects at either end of the spectrum. Hence, there has to be another reality outside that narrow intellectual box.

In the light of such a situation there is therefore the need for a new approach to politics that transcends the existing left/right basis for political activity. The urgency of the call is made by the fact that major future threats are now being compounded rather than resolved by parliamentary governments throughout the advanced industrial world. This is partly because our politicians are only involved or concerned with administrative matters immediately within their grasp, and partly because they are ignorant of or turn a blind eye to the wider implications of the financial-industrial system as it affects the interests of us all.

All political thinking is based on ideological systems which at their birth are usually based on practicable proposals for reform or maintaining the status quo. But with the passing of time and the transformation of society and the world of work, they become outdated, fail to achieve their stated ends, and eventually, as the superstitions of a previous age, lose their credibility entirely. Whilst political superstitions are no less unreasonable than those that are religious or otherwise mystical, they are far more mischievous. Politicians are often aware when their ideologies lose their credibility, but they stick with them all the same for party electoral reasons, whilst resorting to a short-term pragmatism that further compromises their underlying beliefs and compounds those problems they attempt to address.

The first chapter of this book is concerned with revealing how changes in society and the world of work are bringing an end to the left/right conflict as a viable democratic mechanism in advancing the cause of progress. The second chapter is concerned with defining a desirable egalitarian society for freedom and fairness, but it also calls into question the direction of socialist or left-leaning politics. It is shown that socialism is concerned with creating a proletarian rather than an egalitarian society, and because of the missing "gene" of socialism, i.e. its antipathy towards the business ethos, it would be incapable of creating a truly egalitarian society embracing all sectors of the community.

The third and fourth chapters are perhaps the most significant in pinpointing the faults of the financial-industrial system of the advanced industrial economies at the present day, and in exposing the causes responsible for de-industrialisation in threatening the living standards of the many through the enforcement of personal debt. Two forms of capitalism are clearly identified that have been significant in the post-war period: Rentier, based on the rationale of maximising investors' profits; and Productive, based on the priority of maximising market share in fulfilling consumers' needs, and it is the second that is upheld in promoting a sound economy.

The above differentiation of capitalism, however, does not even enter into the consciousness of our rulers, irrespective of the place they occupy in the political spectrum. Instead, they are obsessed by the clash between two failing ideologies: on the one hand, Neo-liberalism or a hazy understanding of capitalism, and on the other, a left-leaning ideology that is generally antipathetic to business. Both sides support so-called globalisation from different perspectives, whilst both give a single interpretation to capitalism to which they are respectively pro or contra. When there is so much misunderstanding it is little wonder there is confusion when it comes to problem solving.

It is generally believed that the industrial decline of the West is traceable to price competition from the East, but such an assertion is quite untrue. The signs of industrial decline in Britain and America were apparent decades before the resurgence of Japan or China. It was the self-destructive effects of Rentier capitalism, or the charging of extortionate interest rates, or usury, that triggered de-industrialisation, although the problem was exacerbated tenfold with the arrival of real competition. As described in this book, leading financiers then compounded a bad situation in a number of ways by piling debt on personal debt.

The fifth chapter is concerned with the Personalisation of Ownership. That is, if "privatisation," or the rule of corporations, is to be brought under control, and left-leaning solutions are equally repudiated because of their anti-business ethos, then there must be another way for ensuring that the financial-industrial system serves the better interests of the majority. And that way is achieved through the democratic accountability of financial power through the democratic means of an emerging individualistic and informed majority, in conjunction with co-determination and realistic employee share-ownership arrangements. This, of course, necessitates prioritising national interests, as international forces are untouchable in the sense that they cannot be made democratically accountable.

The last chapter is concerned with establishing a benign international environment in best serving the needs of all humankind whilst respecting the cultural and economic integrity of different peoples in a very diverse world.

This book is addressed to elected representatives in the advanced industrial economies, both locally and nationally, and irrespective of their place in the political spectrum. Whilst it is equally critical of many established views on both sides of the divides that exist, it also appreciates that most politicians have an underlying understanding of reality that transcends their declared opinions in public, and hence it is this side of their reasoning sensibility that this book seeks to appeal. The book is also addressed to the so-called silent majority, i.e., those thoughtful people who have become disillusioned or alienated from political life due to its deception or self-deception, its hypocrisy, or corruption, or simply due to the fact that it has lost its direction due to events moving ahead at too fast a pace for ordinary understanding.

It should also be noted that such a book as this presenting new ideas, after repudiating entirely the concept of life within the left/right matrix, does raise certain difficulties for the prospective reader. Initially, all new knowledge is perceived in the light of what precedes it through association, and the reader is asked to drive such associations from his mind in properly appreciating the clarity of the new. For example, on one page the views expressed may appear as right wing, whilst on the next they may appear to support the left. The truth, in view of the ultimate structures that emerge, is that such ideas are neither left nor right wing, but something that transcends them both.

This is achieved through syncretism, or the reconciling of differing schools of thought, and can only be fully understood when it is explained that a new ethos is being created for a new society, i.e., new values are presented for the emerging 90% majority, that entail rejecting the values of the old middle and old working classes. To illustrate this, it means that the individual from the emerging majority will at the same time embrace the ethical values ensuring the success of the dynamic business process, whilst equally embracing the holistic values of a society concerned with the welfare of the disadvantaged.

Hence practical ideas for the reform of society necessitate the formation of a new ethical outlook, just as every age involuntarily creates its own distinctive values. Unless the considerate reader appreciates these important factors, the book will be misunderstood and misinterpreted. If the above observations are not taken into account, and the individual is so fixed in his views as to be incapable of adopting or even considering new ideas, then the prospective reader is courteously advised to lay aside this book before embarking on the first chapter.

Most important of all, the book is intended as a catalyst for change, for irrespective of the many proposals that may meet with agreement or scepticism, if it does not succeed in calling for the reform of our financial-industrial system, it will have failed in its purpose. Our libraries are filled with endless books that are critical of our financial-industrial arrangements with which most may agree, but very few that offer constructive proposals. It is in the latter category that this book belongs, and so it opens up a positive discussion on a topic that has not previously been called to public attention.

Whilst summarising the main issues of the topic, every attempt has been made to keep this book as concise as possible and so notes, appendices, and bibliography have not been included. It is hoped that a greatly expanded index will more than compensate as a useful reference source for the omission of the above. Those seriously interested in the arguments presented are urged to consult the *Guide to Further Reading* at the end of the main text for an in-depth explication of the socio-economic principles outlined in the book. The *phony* economy has had its day for far too long. Now is the time to promote the *real* economy.

CONTENTS

CHAPTER 1
The Emergence of Full Democracy

"Without historical thinking, politics turns into a caricature of itself. It is when people possess the capacity to think historically that they can begin to see that their actions can have a significant bearing on their circumstances."

Frank Furedi, *Politics of Fear*, Continuum, 2005, p. 90.

There is a paradox in the present crisis of democracy in the advanced industrial economies in that its cause is not to be found in the possibility of inherent faults, but on the contrary, in the results of its considerable success in resolving major socio-economic issues over the past 60 years. Democracy is best understood as an evolving process together with the advance of society rather than as a description of its supposed function at any particular point in time. This is because the role of democracy is viewed from a different perspective as one decade follows another.

Its origins are clearly traceable to differences between significant socio-economic groups at the apex of society, and arrangements for settling those differences through peaceful means and compromise and the rule of law, rather than through violence, murder, or rebellion. It is inspired and maintained through the idea of freedom, and in its earlier stages it remains a movement *towards democracy* rather than *actual* democracy in itself. It can only arise in societies where property is widely distributed and where trade is established beyond a certain level. The trigger for setting in motion democratic demands or mechanisms is to be found in political situations that are felt as arbitrary or tyrannical in acting against the interests of a significant sector of the population.

The definition of an established democracy is the rule of the majority, howsoever that may be organised, which may be either *Direct*, as in ancient Greece, or through systems of referenda, as in Cantonal Switzerland; or it may be *Representative* through party rule, as in the majority of countries in the modern world. Representative systems may be divided between those that are *Confrontational*, based on dual party systems, as in Britain or America; or *Participatory*, based on the sharing of power through coalitions amongst a number of parties, as in many Continental countries.

The difference between the two main voting systems of *first past the post* and *proportional representation* should also be noted, as a change of system from one to the other may completely transform the political character of a nation state. As a general rule, the first system is applied in Confrontational democracies, whilst the second is found in Participatory democracies. Whilst first past the post tends to harden differences between left and right and discourage the implementation of new ideas; proportional representation, which mainly divides between the systems of the single transferable vote (STV) and mixed member proportional representation (MMP), is generally seen as fairer since it allows significant minorities a share of power.

It is also important to distinguish between *democratic societies* and *democratic government*, for although the latter always includes the former, the obverse does not always follow. A democratic society allows for a large measure of free speech and action, especially in encouraging the full development of the arts and sciences. Thus, in 19th century Europe, Imperial Germany and Austria may be said to have had democratic societies but not democratic governments, even though they had parliaments and electoral systems, because their parliaments were limited by autocratic monarchical authority. Hence voting rights are not sufficient to define democracy, as became plainly clear in the 20th century during the Soviet period. Likewise, ancient Rome, despite the complexity of her electoral system, is not denominated a democracy on the grounds that only certain classes of people could stand for election to specific posts, and by the first century BC was of little help in resolving chronic differences between Patricians and Plebeians, during that troubled period as one civil war followed another.

The industrial, educational and cultural advance of peoples from the 19th century onwards has not therefore always progressed alongside democratic government, although in the West it has usually progressed alongside democratic societies. In the 20th century, Singapore, one of the most advanced industrial economies of the Far East, may be described as a highly successful democratic society, but deficient as a democracy in terms of government. Her academically highly-qualified founders established an authoritarian state with the intention of raising a relatively underdeveloped people to a high level of civilisation within a short period of time, and in this they were entirely successful. It is important to differentiate between an authoritarian and a totalitarian state, for whilst the first allows for a large measure of free thought and action, the latter imposes an ideology detailing as to the desirable way of thinking and style of life.

The first condition for any true democracy, irrespective of whether we refer to its Governmental or Social aspects, is not merely the toleration of free thought and expression through the spoken or written word but its encouragement through its instinctive existence in the cultural environment as well as through established law and the educational system. Following on from this as a logical consequence must be the right to free action by individuals or groups providing no harm comes to others or their property, or that which belongs to the common interest, or the environment, or entails self-harm. Free speech or other modes of expression should be unrestricted as it touches on any aspect of ideas or things unless it leads directly to a breach of the peace or to damage or the loss of property, or is liable to do so.

Such definitions of the misuse of free speech naturally give rise to controversy. Such misuse may only be properly judged in the light of a society's situation at a particular time in its history. For example, the flagrant use of the Swastika may amount in Germany to a justifiably criminal act in view of the sensibilities of that country in the light of the recent past; whilst the similar use of the Swastika in neighbouring or other countries may be dismissed as eccentricity or the aberrant act of a disordered mind, calling for little more than public reprehension.

Controversy may also arise on what is likely to cause a breach of the peace, and this should be decided by public opinion and the courts not according to subjective views on the offensiveness of the opinions, or those expressing them, but rather according to the factual evidence of past riots or law-breaking that have occurred through the expression of similar outbursts. In such decision-making, freedom of speech should not be restricted merely on the assumed grounds of "protecting a group from being offended." This is a topical issue and comes under the general heading of "political correctness."

Over the past years, university student bodies have banned or cancelled the speaking engagements of a wide variety of scholars (some of them eminent in the public sphere) on the grounds that their line of thinking would cause offence to the "young minds" of those addressed. The real reason for the suppression of such free speech is not to protect the susceptibilities of "young minds," but rather to censor the political or other opinions that student leaders find objectionable. It may be that a minority of such student audiences have extreme or violent views and are prepared – as demonstrated by past events – to use violence in physically attempting to eject such speakers from their platform. But the prospect of such a threat is not a sufficient justification in itself for the suppression of free speech.

Political Correctness is the new movement in the advanced industrial world for either the displacement of harsh realities, so that euphemisms may replace more honest or direct expressions; or for the suppression of free opinion when tensions extend beyond a certain point between conflicting groups. Although appreciation should be given to the fact that words change their meaning or emphasis over a period of time, political correctness overrides such considerations in deferring to sensibilities in forcing a change of attitudes simply through manipulating the language. Examples of using euphemisms in displacing harsher realities are the following, when such words as Bad Behaviour, Retarded and Cripple, have been replaced respectively by, Challenging, Learning Difficulty, or Disabled. In the second category, alternative descriptive labels, supposedly more complementary, are given to various racial or other groups.

Furthermore, any such generalisations applied to groups deemed to be minorities that are discriminated against, are considered as prejudicial simply on the grounds that they are stereotypical labels, and irrespective of their factual authenticity as generalisations. The word "stereotypical" has falsely been turned into a pejorative term in the sense of prejudicial, or casting a bad light on an object when it is seen as objectionable.

Political correctness is motivated by a patronising attitude, and although its moral intention may be laudable, it is demeaning to the dignity of those to whom it is applied. In a truly democratic environment all should be treated as equal and of equal worth in sharing the culture of a society. If minorities are to receive true acceptance by the majority, then candid relationships dictate that the latter should not adopt an artificial special regard, or pretence by politicians, for that leads inescapably to misunderstanding that eventually will be uncovered – usually through bad-tempered outbursts when a lid is pressed down on a boiling pot. It should further be added that such inventions create a bar between differing groups, for differences that are real should be appreciated for what they are rather than hidden or abhorred. The ultimate bane of political correctness is that it creates a web of deceit throughout society, and this in itself is an attack on freedom if the latter is contingent on personal integrity.

In the pre-industrial age, those territories moving towards a democratic direction, e.g., the City states of Italy or the Low Countries, or the Hanse and other isolated cities in Germany, were oligarchies rather than democracies, as their majorities were not usually included in sharing power. It was only with the advent of the industrial revolution, towards the close of the 18th century, that entire populations were eventually to become involved in the democratic process: at first through the rise of the revolutionary left, and then from the close of the 19th century, the emergence of socialist-like movements in representative bodies. Hence, without the industrial revolution Full Democracy would and could never have evolved. Ideas for freedom and justice do not spontaneously arise in the minds of people through their social conscience. They are forced into existence through economic circumstances.

Democracy cannot exist without differences between groups as to right or wrong policies or as to their interpretation. As soon as the conflict over differences vanish, then democracy is at an end. A fully developed democracy, i.e., involving all sectors of the population, is anticipated by its participants to be long-lasting on the assumption that change and progress is never-ending, but the actuality of its permanence may be quite another matter.

The purpose of democracy is not merely to fulfil the will of populations at any one point in time, but more significantly, to fulfil the potential of humankind in the face of unanticipated difficulties that may arise in the future. In enabling such mental flexibility, in meeting the unexpected demands of progress, it is therefore necessary that democracy should be ideologically free of prejudice or fixed ideas of any kind. Consequently, ethics should be based on utilitarian and universal values, and in conserving the essence of a culture, essential for maintaining the identity of a people, new interpretations are necessarily given to established beliefs. In this role, democracy may be seen as a creative life-giving dynamic for the progress of society.

For the past 200 years' the left/right conflict or class divide, has served as the mechanism in driving forward democracy. It has acted as a dialectic, i.e., as a process in uncovering supposed truths for the betterment of the general population. The unknown becomes the beneficial solution for the future, so that each succeeding age is marked by new ideals or policies to be achieved, and there is always a tension between the old and the new and between one generation and the next.

Hence the need for democracy to avoid entrapment in rigid ideological systems that might frustrate this process, for even the most conservative sectors of society are forced to adapt to change with the passing of time. The extremism of both poles within the political spectrum is eroded by the acceptance of the new, and whilst revolutionaries become moderates in their middle years, ultra-conservatives end their lives by embracing ideals that might have outraged their parents or their younger selves.

If that is the historical view of progress over the longer term, a snapshot view of democracy at a particular point in time presents a very different picture. Here we see quarrelling opposing parties with entrenched views, sticking with fixed ideas in their determination to overcome the opposition by whatever means. Conflict self-generates its own antagonism, especially when it needs to uphold the justice of its cause, and when compromise is reached it is often as a survival strategy rather than as a surrender to unwelcome decisions – and those decisions, in objective terms, are not necessarily the wisest, even for the medium term.

The livelihood of the parliamentary politician is dependent on votes, and votes are dependent on the politicians supposed loyalty to the party in the eye of electors, as well as upon the whips who ensure the politicians' loyalty to the leadership. All this helps to secure the values of parties in themselves as well as to the communities they serve, and so ideological factors are called upon to strengthen belief. If belief diminishes there is resort to pretence, or if it is lost entirely, then pragmatism is evoked on a day-to-day basis, but always the party remains the anchor for political activity.

Due to the intensity of party struggle, and because of the concentration on short-term ends, the politician is hardly conscious of democracy as a long-term process. His primary concern is with the ends of socialism or the ends of conservatism, or some other ideological fixation, rather than with the broader or more abstract idea of progress which he may be loathed or incapable of defining. He is a man or woman of action, disdaining theory, and hence has the making of a poor philosopher or sociologist. And this helps explain the present crisis of democracy.

We have stated that democracy cannot exist without differences between groups, or the interpretation of those differences, and here we must emphasise that such differences should be real in economic terms and not merely invented. Democracy as class struggle between left and right has served as an ideal medium for 200 years in driving forward progress, as those differences were perceived as injustice and oppression which the stronger or authoritarian class may have attempted to disguise as the natural condition of humankind. In pre-industrial times the underclass were always oppressed according to modern interpretations of fairness, although they may have accepted their condition with fatalism as God-given, only occasionally rising in revolt in times of famine or pandemics, or other apocalyptic disasters, and usually they were finally crushed by those in established authority.

The millennia of humankind in accepting passively the divisions of class as an inevitable condition of society came finally to an end with the emergence of the industrial revolution. This occurred through the widespread dispossession of the majority from their small-scale family-sized productive enterprises, and self-sustainable plots, and enforcement into an alienated proletarian status through the rise of ever-larger modes for manufacturing essential and other marketable products. Thus, an underclass that may have been independent although poor or limited in resources, suffered the indignity of losing that independence in becoming the wage earners of an absolute master who might dismiss them at will. This economic process began as far back as the 1530s with the sack of the monasteries, but only accelerated fast, as noted above, with industrialisation towards the close of the 18th century.

In this way, class consciousness as a distinct political concept touching every sector for the population came into being, and with it, the distant realisation that egalitarianism of some kind might or should be a possibility sometime in the future. The most violent expression of this was experienced through the French Revolution in 1789, whilst in the calmer environment of other nation states, democratic associations and parliamentary movements emerged to legislate for greater fairness and opportunity for the economically oppressed majority. These changes may be seen as the most significant turning point in the history of humankind.

But class consciousness on this scale was a two-way process for it evoked a defensive reaction from those better placed in society. Entrenched positions arose as a spontaneous reaction to the widening divide, and so the left/right conflict came into being as a democratic mechanism for settling differences. Until the early 1960s class differences were evident on many levels: visually through clothing styles and condition; housing and living standards; accent and mode of speaking; leisure pursuits, etc. Mutual dislike, motivated by both fear and envy, saw the cultural emergence of two conflicting classes, usually referred to as the bourgeoisie versus the proletariat, and each had their own pride and separate values. The politically silent majority, in its greater wisdom, may have found this divide not merely distasteful but de-humanising, senseless, and intolerable for the eventual improvement of humankind.

It may be that this silent majority, in conjunction with the unspoken better nature of those in politics, exerted a greater influence on the future than the clash of ideologies. In any event, the following decades experienced the transformation of society and the world of work. This was achieved through increasingly democratic legislation; the extension of ever-more rights to the general population as well as to formerly under-privileged minorities; fairer and better conditions in the workplace; and a more open society where secretiveness was seen as a conspiracy against freedom. In the advanced industrial economies, the conditions of life and work of those in the 21st century bore a distant relationship to those in the 1960s. A new egalitarianism had emerged in terms of the diminution of material differences and the broadening of opportunity.

With the emergence of a new majority absorbing those at the polar ends of society, the old middle and working classes were fast disappearing as significant sectors of the community. And new values followed inevitably in the wake of this. Individualism supplanted Collectivism not out of voluntary choice but through the necessity in meeting the demands of increasing occupational differentiation. Children no longer, as a matter of course, followed in the footsteps of parents, for with the widening of occupational opportunities and the greater demand on brainpower, choice and ability became the great decider of future prospects. All these differences widened the divide between the generations, for the new occupations arising from robotisation and information technology, etc., were meaningless and incomprehensible to the older half of the population. Whilst the self-assurance and pride in status of the older middle class was eroded by the shifting tectonic plates of society; the shoulder-to-shoulder collectivism of the older working class was ridiculed in reflecting the attitudes of a passing age.

When, therefore, the majority population were called upon by their political leaders to "do battle" against the class enemy, however tactfully this appeal may have been disguised, the response was apathy, disdain, or even disgust. Why should enmity be aroused where none was felt? What sense was there in a "War cry" that might have been valid 60 years earlier but was now of no value in a world that had been transformed? The anticipated outcome was that party memberships across the political spectrum collapsed, as also did voting figures. The majority had become alienated from the democratic system when ideology stopped in its tracks whilst the actuality of progress continued along its path.

The emerging middle majority remained a highly heterogeneous class, without as yet a distinctive mind-set or sense of direction. But all that was destined to change. Its withdrawal from participation in parliamentary politics was but the first step. Despite the cultural differences that divided the various sections of this middle majority, there were nonetheless underlying socio-economic interests that coalesced towards a common political direction. These will be analysed in the chapters below. Here we are only concerned with identifying the futility of the left/right struggle as a mechanism in advancing the progress of society.

In a society that is egalitarian or speeding towards a greater degree of egalitarianism, the will of the majority is towards a state of unity. If men and women are called to fight one another over issues where they see no reasonable grounds for conflict, then they will not be led or misled by those purporting to be their leaders. When material standards have reached a satisfactorily sufficient level for the 90% majority, then politics dependent on discriminating between the Haves and Have-nots loses its attraction. Those in the lower occupational grades with sufficient funds in their pockets for fulfilling their needs will cease to envy those who are more affluently placed.

In an aspirational egalitarian society the more lowly enjoy a healthy ambition for the future with no consciousness that the more prosperous are in any way oppressors. Likewise, the more affluent will cease to fear the more-lowly as a threat to their status or the seizure of their possessions. These positive attitudes are dependent on a feeling of fairness throughout all levels of the community on the political conditions of life.

The 90% new majority may be described as a classless society in the sense that it stands alone unthreatened by an electorally significant population sector intent on its overthrow or submission to an alternative style of authority. In such a society 2 ½% may be categorised as the super-rich and 7 ½% as an underclass. Both sectors are heterogeneous in that the underclass does not comprise a proletariat as understood in a pre-1960s world, but rather an assortment of unfortunates from every level of the community, as the insolvent or bankrupt, addicts of alcohol, drugs or gambling, ex-prisoners, the disabled, and different categories of the mentally unstable. Meanwhile, those at the apex of society would have derived their wealth from legitimate or illegal modes of business, or from the arts or sport, or the skilled manipulation of financial resources. Because of their diversity, neither those at the top or the bottom of society, would present a natural political bloc, and even if they did organise politically, their numbers would remain electorally insignificant.

The terms Egalitarianism and Class need further elucidation. Egalitarianism suggests reducing or increasing the population to an agreed desired level, but if by this is meant the enforcing measures of an extreme left wing or Communist state, as in Pol Pott's Cambodia or pre-1978 China, where all were dressed in a standard form of civilian clothing, that would present an intolerable situation. Maximising equality of opportunity, in so far as that is practicable, is not sufficient in defining egalitarianism. There must also be an agreed level of minimum material standards; and thirdly, a cultural or educational level in facilitating an easy mode of communication in conveying the parameters of fairness in society to which the majority assent. The Full Democracy of an advanced industrial economy would entail aspirational egalitarianism without which freedom cannot exist.

This necessitates that each individual should seek to maximise his or her full potential as a personality, and develop latent abilities to their fullest extent. This should be motivated primarily by internal interests as seen by the individual, and only secondarily in view of a competitive social environment. If the striving for self-improvement is motivated purely through competition with one's peers, as too often occurs in certain parts of the New World, this too frequently leads to the corruption or debasement of values, and the undermining of those cultural qualities unifying society, as well as to the adoption of undesirable stereotypical tendencies. The prime purpose of self-improvement should be the unique creativity of the individual as an end in himself and not the desire for enslaving conformity.

Aspirational egalitarianism should not generate envy or fear but appreciation of the value of *difference* as the unique quality of each individual. Thus, each individual may be allowed to rise or fall, or otherwise change, within the desirable margins of material living standards, without loss of status in the eyes of those around him. Such attitudes would be well supported by the huge variety of means that individuals choose to use their personal material resources. Wealth or affluence cannot be measured purely through its display in a world where the relatively lowly are often the hoarders of mounds of possessions, whilst many of the wealthy lead a mean or miserly existence. In an acceptably egalitarian society with a high level of culture, a provocative display of riches would anyway be despised as vulgarity, and so too would the miser be disdained for his meanness to himself and family.

Aspirational egalitarianism, or egalitarianism of the free society, allows for the upward or downward movement in society without cause for pain or undue self-congratulation on the assumption that society is both equal and democratic. In such a society of the 90% majority there would be no socio-political barriers to prevent ease of communication, or even socialising, between those from any level of the community. We can already recognise the emergence of such a society in the 21st century.

Furthermore, it may be asserted that all mainstream parliamentary parties, irrespective of their place within the political spectrum, throughout the advanced industrial world, already outwardly support the right to equality of opportunity, the right to a decent standard of living, and the right to state assistance in the event of personal disaster. Such rights would not have been upheld by mainstream parliamentary parties 150 years ago, when resort to charitable institutions or the Work House were the only alternatives. If there is a political progress of attitudes, this is always followed within a generation or two by complementary political action.

The definition of a Full Democracy is therefore a society in which the new middle majority has not only realised its full consciousness as an economic interest group (as defined in the following chapters), but has ascended to power through democratic means. It embraces the interests of all society, irrespective of occupation or status, and since it is not electorally threatened by rival class interests, it has a generous attitude to the disadvantaged and a fearless attitude to the super-rich. The basis for its democratic struggle for better socio-economic conditions, without which democracy cannot be maintained, will be presented in the fifth chapter.

CHAPTER 2
Defining Egalitarianism

"The mill-workers, coal-miners and flower sellers who spent their time producing Shakespeare plays and reading classic works of literature did not think that literature was part of someone else's culture. On the contrary ... they believed in an idea of relevance far more broad-minded than the narrow and crippling one we have in schools today. Shakespeare, Dickens and Milton *were* relevant to them."

Daisy Christodoulou, *Seven Myths about Education*,
Routledge, 2014, p. 119.

The question of Class must be treated as something quite separate from that of Egalitarianism, and this is because of the ideological consequences of the left/right conflict. Socialists and all those on the left claim that their struggle is for a Classless society, but this is something they would be incapable of achieving due to an inescapable bias.

This is demonstrated on two counts: firstly, through the consistent ideology of socialism, and secondly, through the historical records of those socialist societies established in Eastern Europe and elsewhere. What those on the left really seek to establish is a proletarian or Working Class society, and that is quite different from an egalitarian society embracing an entire population with its varied and conflicting interests.

A working class ethos is not only in conflict with middle class values on many counts, but is also in conflict with the psychological dynamism necessary for a business culture to flourish. We may examine these differences as separate spheres of belief. The idealisation of the working class arose through the natural battle lines that came into existence and a set of cultural values that subsequently fell into place. The assertion justifying the working class cause began with the assumption of its virtuous position, or at least, moral supremacy over other sectors of the community stemming from this, implicitly supported by Biblical and Christian values. Karl Marx was descended from a long line of eminent Rabbis, and his influence by the Old Testament, perhaps the greatest study of resentment in world literature, is always evident in his writing. The story of a minority oppressed by Oriental monarchies, invading from several directions, and their single-minded belief in a monotheistic deity to finally resolve their predicament, presented an exact paradigm for so-called scientific socialism. The Christianity of the New Testament – Marx was brought up in the Lutheran faith from early childhood – added to this line of thinking, with the promise of a new world, whilst also assenting to the authority of the secular realm.

When the left identified the bourgeoisie as the class enemy they needed to blacken its reputation not merely as an unintentional oppressor but as a moral evil, for only ethical forces would have the authority and permanence to carry the battle to its conclusion. Hence, whilst the solidarity of collectivism was portrayed as socially laudable in promoting progress; individualism was portrayed as self-centredness leading to the destruction of a unified and philanthropic society. The values of the working class were even extended to modes of oral speaking, manners, and style of dress, as otherwise the adoption of middle class ways might be interpreted as class betrayal. Consequently, even those from the middle class supporting socialist doctrines adopted subtle changes to their behaviour and appearance.

When intellectually minded socialists are confronted with the shortcomings of endorsing proletarian culture, they usually respond defensively by arguing that proletarianism is a changing process, and so is not necessarily fixed in stereotypical views from a past age. This argument may be valid, but it raises two points: firstly, what is the value of promoting proletarian values in the light of hoping for transforming material standards in the near future;? and secondly, whenever party tensions are exacerbated, e.g., during election periods, then the left always turn with duplicity to the bad old images that existed decades earlier.

If proletarianism is promoted as an end in itself, this raises two inter-connected questions: firstly, how can aspirational values be properly advanced;? and secondly, is not the underclass being deprived of the hope for all the better things in life through its attachment to such an ideology? The answer to the first question is simply that the expression of aspirational values would entail stepping out of line, and that would contradict the principle of egalitarianism. The second question is more interesting. If the better things of life are only to be enjoyed by the privileged or affluent, does this place them in a category of moral condemnation?

In the eyes of socialists such things are usually regarded with mild disdain, or else simply dismissed with the neutral comment as "not for us." This attitude is dictated by incomprehension rather than moral obloquy. In any event, it amounts to the repudiation of cultural values and activities, and in doing so uses class prejudice as an excuse for plain ignorance and disdain. We are here referring to the enjoyment of such varied things as good wine and food, opera, great literature, painting, culturally explorative foreign travel, study of other languages, and specialised sports such as golf, fives, and polo, etc., and even to the expression of intelligence in a general sense. In regard to the latter, it may be noted that "speaking above the heads" of one's associates is even disdained by the middle class – even if unintentionally.

An example demonstrating proletarian attitudes to the hard evidence of materialism may be illustrated by the following story. When Raphael Samuel (of more shortly) visited East Germany with a party of Communist comrades at the start of the 1950s, their hosts took them on a bus tour into West Berlin for a visual comparison between the two great divisions of the world. The universal conclusion of the group, irrespective of what may have been the true or hidden opinion of their hosts, was that here was decadence on display expressed through the self-indulgence of hedonistic materialism.

The bright lights and luxury restaurants of the Ku'damm was merely evidence of a degenerate and selfish population with no thought for the higher values of a proletarian existence. How much more preferable and peaceful were the modest half-lit streets of East Berlin with their uncrowded environment, where the people enjoyed the comforts of home life rather than the hellish noise of vulgar entertainment! Such is the power of ideology in transforming the evidence of prosperity into an image of the undesirable society.

The ingrained stubbornness, intentional or otherwise, and the arrogant (almost religious) self-righteousness of proletarianism in despising the joyful things of life does not contribute to a desirable egalitarian society. In the name of ensuring equality such better things could be banished by the state, and in citing an extreme case, in accordance with this principle, all those who wore spectacles in Pol Pott's Cambodia were put up against a wall and shot as an intellectual threat to the conformity of the population. The greatest underlying psychological threat of the left to the development of a free and prosperous society is resentment against those who feel they are oppressed by their "betters," and such an affliction has little to do with those from any particular level in society. Such resentment is rather traceable to early influences of family upbringing, and so as many may be found amongst the affluent as amongst the poor, and consequently many from all levels of society will be drawn to support the left as their naturally comfortable political home.

A far more logical approach of the left to the problem of class oppression would not have been the idealisation of proletarianism (or the proletariat) but the idealisation of the material standards of those placed at the centre of society. Such an approach could not be effectively advanced in "revolutionary" terms, but it would be based on common sense. It would entail the repudiation of the values of the aristocracy or the new super-rich, in favour of a middling affluence and comfortable standard of life. But such a stance might nonetheless continue, in certain circumstances, to offer a threat to left-leaning values.

When the middle classes first emerged in the 16th and 17th centuries as a distinct population sector, and chose to distinguish themselves from the ruling landed nobility, it was not with a resentful *untertan* attitude. It was manifested firstly through a religious Puritanism and the purging of idols and superstition and other barriers between themselves and God, and secondly through the business of work and money-making in the service of God. In this way, they separated their values and interests from the ruling authorities, and eventually, in England and elsewhere this led to civil conflict.

At a later stage in history, from the 18th century onwards, a different pattern emerged in their relationships. The upper middle classes in England aspired to a landownership status in imitation of the aristocracy. From the late 19th century onwards this proved to be a malign cultural influence, since it diluted the energy and purpose of the manufacturing class in contributing to rentier financial tendencies. This is a topic that the eminent

American historian, Martin Wiener, studied in depth in his book, *English Culture and the Decline of the Industrial Spirit.* Hence, if proletarian or working class values should be repudiated, so too should the values of the old middle class in favour of the new emerging 90% middle majority. The above illustrates how differing class divisions influence society in a variety of ways.

In returning to the question of proletarianism at the present day if resentment is an undesirable characteristic of the left, its most significant and dangerous psychological attitude is its response to enterprise. The left's repudiation or blindness to the necessity for dynamism in allowing business culture to flourish is the greatest divide between left and right. The question of the dynamic of healthy business enterprise has nothing to do with the principle of right or wrong, but rather is interpreted as bureaucracy versus the natural business process. This is not to infer that business is not confronted by huge problems in serving the better interests of the majority, but such problems are only hazily perceived by those on the left and these will be discussed in the following chapter of this book. The left fail to understand the nature of business, and in their incomprehension, they approach the "monster" with a mixture of disdain and fear, applying bureaucratic cures that impede its progress and stem its freedom.

The suspicion of business, as the fear of the "unknown," is something that extends beyond the world of politics, but it becomes politically significant in the realm of government. The apparent irrationality of business, particularly in times of economic crisis, is a cause of fear amongst all sectors of the population. There are those with a business sense and those without it. Those with a "nose" for business have a natural aptitude for money-making, and tend to arouse a sense of discomfort amongst those more attuned to duller or more comprehensible occupations. Business is a creative activity, similar to art, and whilst the artist produces paintings or sculptures which inexplicably have beauty, the businessman produces profits which are disdained because their value is not so easily seen.

But why should the products of beauty be held in higher regard than those of profit when the latter facilitate the means not only for our physical survival, but well-being and prosperity in every sphere of material life? Is it that spiritual well-being should be placed on a pedestal whilst material well-being should be despised? This may be in accordance with a false religiosity, but it conflicts entirely with promoting the good of all humankind.

There is a need to revive our entire value system. There are civilisations that lay greater moral emphasis on business enterprise, and others that are more entrenched in the moral service to the state, and the latter are always driven by their military origins. The Chinese and Semitic civilisations were (and are) predominantly business cultures, and so too were the ancient Greeks and their modern descendants. As business or trade is in itself a free activity, all other forms of social freedom were to spring from this. Democracy, that rare form of majority government, has only sprung from business dominated societies, but that is not to suggest that an enterprise environment usually leads to a democratic society for it plainly does not.

Western civilisation, on the other hand, if it is dated from early Roman times, has been predominantly service based on a military infrastructure until the recent past. Historians have dated the deciding event in 146 BC with the destruction of Carthage and her business-oriented Semitic people. Until that time the three destructive Punic wars had taken place in the Western Mediterranean between two contrasting civilisations, and with the victory of Rome, the military ethos was to survive in differing forms until the recurring conflicts of the West European nations early in the 16th century which led to the development of a new business culture, and eventually to democracy.

As a final observation on this comparison between enterprise and military-dominated civilisations an interesting contrast may be noted between China and the Russian Federation at the present time. The transformation of China between 1978 and the present may have astonished the world, but it was an episode that could have been anticipated. Here was an extreme left wing regime which had experienced the horrors of the Great Leap Forward, with the millions who had perished through famine, and later underwent the tyrannical reforms of the Cultural Revolution, metamorphosing its existence into the most modern of capitalistic nation states whilst nominally retaining its Communist credentials.

The explanation, of course, is to be found in the fact that the dragon awoke from a long slumber of several hundred years, after a millennium or two of active commercial enterprise in addition to placing the value of education on a high level for the many. That, in addition to the practical values of Confucianism, deeply implanted in the Chinese people, was to ensure their success when they awoke from the sleep that had isolated them from the rest of the world.

In contrast, when the Wall came down in East Berlin, and the East bloc gained its freedom, there was joy throughout Western Europe that Russia might at last gain it freedom and be integrated into the brother- and sisterhood of the advanced industrial economies of the West. But it was not to be. Russia collapsed into chaos, and those who had been the guardians of state enterprise, seized the means of production, distribution, and exchange, for their own ends, and sank into a bloodthirsty mafia, in a country where the rule of law had vanished. When eventually the situation calmed, the country settled into an economically unhappy dictatorship of gloom and pauperism. Why was this?

The Russian people had always comprised an enslaved majority since the time of the Mongol invasions in the 13th century. The Soviet regime was no better than the Tsarist era that preceded it if the slaughter of 25 million for political motives is taken into consideration during Stalin's rule. Until 1862, the majority lived without property in ignorant serfdom, and the only consolation of the people was (and still is) the promise of the Orthodox church for a better hereafter. All this demonstrates that the heritage of a people decides its future, and that a business culture is one of the greatest blessings with which any nation may be endowed.

The changing approach of the Labour party in Britain to the world of business over the past 100 years is something that must be noted. In the early 20th century the primary topic of conversation in Labour party circles was the nature of capitalism and the need for radical reform. In the 21st century, in Labour party circles, the subject of capitalism has become a taboo topic. What happened in the intervening period? The rot began to set in in the early 1930s with Ramsay MacDonald's coalition government and its fall, and his betrayal and expulsion from the Labour party. After 1945, with the election of Clement Attlee, the City institutions re-organised after the War in ensuring their entrenchment and domination as never before. The consequences of this will be examined in the subsequent chapters of this book, for here we are only concerned with the Labour party and its relationship with the financial-industrial system. An informal agreement was reached between the Labour party and the financial institutions that each would go their own way if neither interfered with the other.

This was a satisfactory arrangement on the superficial level, for the party embarked on the greatest social reforms of the century, with the establishment of the NHS and better measures in protecting pensioners, the unemployed, and those who had otherwise fallen upon hard times. Meanwhile, Nationalisation policies had success in some directions but failure in others, as power was not directly passed onto the shoulders of working people, but into the hands of a remote middle class elite, and this gave rise to misunderstanding and resentment. Hence, from 1945 until the present day, governments of the left have concerned themselves with reforms, mostly on the margins of society, whilst leaving a completely free hand to the capitalist system and this has proved disastrous to the national economy if comparisons are made with our toughest industrial competitors.

In the words of the economic historian, Prof. Sidney Pollard, in the immediate Post-War period, "the City took over again: this time it had a different composition, in which an immensely powerful Treasury, the Economics establishment and much else joined the financiers, now a much stronger element in society. The world was treated to the spectacle of a once powerful industrial economy being hit on the head again and again in the pursuit of policies dictated by the tiny segment of the City, and in the process dropping from being the leading economic power in Europe at the end of the War to one of its weakest, and from one of the richest countries to one of the poorest." (*The Neglect of Industry: A critique of British Economic Policy since 1870*, Erasmus University, Rotterdam, 1984, pp. 15-16.)

The last significant occasion when the Labour party distanced itself from the world of business, in shedding its responsibility for majority interests, was in 1997 with the decision to devolve the setting of monetary policy to a committee, known as the Monetary Policy Committee, comprising nine economists at the Bank of England. And this decision was taken without even a mention in the ruling Labour party's pre-election manifesto.

If the above paragraphs present the political stance of the left's approach to the secret world of the financial institutions, something more must be said about the cultural outcome of class attitudes as broadly influenced by left-leaning academia, together with the media and the political establishment. The declared intention of creating a classless society was doubtless made in all sincerity, but the chosen means was not merely unsuitable but destined to frustrate the desired end. The moves to create a proletarian or working class society, whether intended or unconscious, was not merely the task of the organised parliamentary left.

Far more significant were the efforts of academia through the influence of Cultural Marxism, which in the decades following the War, was to become a powerful force in universities worldwide. Cultural Marxism naturally puts emphasis on proletarianism as of value in itself, without questioning as to whether it would lead to the creation of an egalitarian society. As the bourgeoisie was identified as the class enemy, it was assumed that the triumph of the working class was the only possible alternative. No thought was given to the transformation of society through the emergence of a New Majority or its outcome, or the consequent need to repudiate both the middle and working class philosophies of life, and everything associated with the left/right conflict.

Cultural Marxism did not so much emerge through a declared political philosophy as through the historical research of a historian – albeit with firm Communist views. Raphael

Samuel, described by the cultural theorist, Stuart Hall, as "one of the most outstanding, original intellectuals of his generation," was amongst the most prominent advocates of Cultural Marxism, initially as the co-founder of the journal, *Past and Present* in 1952, that pioneered the study of working class history, and later as the founder of the *History Workshop*, a research movement known as studying "history from below." He was subsequently the author of numerous articles and a number of books on the same topic. I knew Samuel well at the start of the 1950s, when he was a year ahead of me, and we were rivals in the debating society at King Alfred School.

At that time he was a fervent Stalinist, a loyalty he publicly repudiated to all and sundry in 1956 after the Hungarian uprising. My attitude, then as now, was to reject class-based politics as de-humanising and in distorting the reality of substantive issues. The de-humanising aspects of class war was something I had already witnessed and even experienced in all its horror several years earlier, as described in my autobiography, *This Was My England the story of a Childhood*.

The intensity of my arguments with Samuel ensured that we were the most prominent participants in the debating society, and when I was elected its leader, under the watchful eye of the headmistress, Hettie Barber, mother of the famous jazz band leader, Chris Barber, Samuel protested loudly that my forte was "history and not politics," but he was unable to overturn the majority vote – and anyway, the grounds of his objection were irrelevant to the decision as the society was also engaged in topics beyond those of politics.

Samuel was a master in the use of ridicule, which for the most part kept hostility within the bounds of civilised exchange, but on one occasion when publicly asserting that the father of one of the participants was a "Troskyist," it touched a raw nerve that led to a blazing row that went beyond the school gates. Several teachers were involved in mending the situation, and finally Samuel was obliged to offer a formal apology. Samuel had originally intended to embark on a political career, but the history master, John Handford (who later worked for the UCL), persuaded him to become an academic. In following this advice he became far more influential in promoting proletarianism in educational circles worldwide and through the intelligentsia, than he could ever have been as a member of parliament on the far left.

The prime critique of Cultural Marxism is that it defers to the lesser values of proletarianism, and so unquestionably frustrates the successful achievement of an upwardly aspiring egalitarianism. Its fixture on the idea that working class values are somehow "better" or more "virtuous" than those of any other sector of the population, even if not openly declared, is simply false or based on illusion. The idea may be based on biblical sources, as noted above, and may also be reflected in the writings of such prominent authors as Dickens or Dostoyevsky. There is, however, a more significant aspect of this topic in that poverty and oppression corrupts the character in driving it towards crime and wrongdoing rather than in embellishing it towards goodness and philanthropy. This is not to suggest that the comfortable affluent are in their turn free from malice, but they are more commonly prone to the sin of complacency. It would be more correct, therefore, to suggest that all individuals have faults of character, of one kind or another, irrespective of their origins or status.

Closely associated with Cultural Marxism is the influence of Post-modernism, the greatest intellectual poison of all to afflict the second half of the 20th century, and still widely influential at the present time. Post-modernism may have some validity in the discussion of contemporary schools of modern art, but when it is carried over to the social sciences it is wholly malign. The relativism that argues that no priority of value can be given to anything, or that objectivity is something that cannot be considered, not only destroys the possibility for intelligent discussion, but repudiates 3,000 years of philosophical thought. It does serve as an aid, however, to the idea that proletarianism may be a value in itself and that all opposition to such a concept may be dismissed without reason. Post-modernism when applied to the social sciences is a thuggish weapon which pushes forward any nonsense it chooses if rationality has otherwise been exhausted.

All societies and nation states need therefore to set standards to which all should defer, and in the full democracy of advanced industrial economies, these should aim at a desirable egalitarianism. If equality of opportunity is to be made a reality and not merely an empty promise, as at present, then the individual has the right to be educated in such a way as to find acceptability in any social milieu. This means that education should be so extended that the schoolchild should be taught social skills to even include the etiquette of table manners at lunchtime, or received pronunciation and correct spoken as well as written grammar, in the same way that High German is taught throughout the German speaking world, so that those from different territories might meet and more easily communicate as equals, as without these qualities it would be difficult to move easily in the most affluent, educated, or successful circles. If there is sincerity in the promise of "equality of opportunity" then it should not be offered without the preparation or tools for its fulfilment.

The entertainment, media and advertising industries are clearly the most blameworthy of all in appealing to the lowest possible denominator. In deferring to the most simplistic taste an insult is not merely given to the less affluent part of the population, but to every man, woman and child irrespective of status. One has merely to pick up any magazine advertising radio or TV programmes to be disillusioned by what is on offer. The cult of celebrity is especially distasteful in its banality and drawing attention, for no particular reason, to the same personalities week after week, for lack of any more meaningful topics to cover. The high ideals of John Reith, first Director-General of the BBC, to "inform, educate and entertain," have long gone out of the window. Note should especially be taken of the remarks of the forthright late Labour MP, Gwilym Roberts, when he condemned pop music as the "new and deadly opium of the masses," and that it was ruining young people's mental health – assertions that should be given much greater research and credibility in the cause of promoting an aspirational egalitarian society for the future.

The only point of Cultural Marxism as it influences the social sciences, that I can discern, is as a weapon in its perpetuation of the class war in attacking middle and upper class values, but even if it emerged victorious, it would leave the majority population culturally impoverished. Its negative view of so many aspects of life, with the inevitable even if unintended consequence of downgrading high culture, would diminish the lives of us all. In such an environment, a form of "political correctness" would emerge as a reminder as to which activities, sources of enjoyment, or modes of thought were acceptable or non-acceptable. A form of undeclared censorship would be imposed, condemning association with huge swathes of culture to a status of non-recognition. And the repercussions of such an environment would inevitably diminish many areas of material as well as intellectual progress, as has already been demonstrated in an East European world that is no more.

The problem with Marxism and all subsequent left-leaning thinking from which it drew, is that Marx eschewed the idea of prediction or describing an actual socialist society. He condemned such an attempt as absurd or utopian, and confined his intellectual exploration to the pseudo-science of dialectical and historical materialism. The problem of the socialist imagination, and the cowardice entailed in declining to picture in realistic terms the socialist society has led to all kinds of absurdities. It is easy enough to envisage proletarian values whilst living in a middle class dominated society, but witness the embarrassment if that society collapsed, and the left finally emerged as the victors in the class war. Would they then have embarked on constructing a proletarian society in a West European environment? It is doubtful, and the viability of engaging in such a project is even more remote.

It may be argued that the proletariat, or what remains of the working class that have yet to be integrated into the 90% New Majority, have a natural right to the populism that appeals to their taste, and moreover, that it necessarily fulfils their democratic rights. There will always be some controversy on where a line should be drawn between the moral obligation of the better informed to impose their higher cultural standards on the less fortunate, and the right of the latter to enjoy the banality of "populist" pleasures. The issue is indeed a moral one on two counts: firstly, because the imposition of such standards is made in the cause of creating a more egalitarian society on the aspirational model; and secondly, because populism is in itself demeaning to the personality when higher aspirations would uplift the latter.

The last point may be vividly illustrated by the fact that in the contemporary world there would be universal condemnation of the torture and slaughter of hundreds of animals in a stadium, and yet that was the "populist" pleasure offered the proletariat by the Roman authorities. There is only a matter of degree between that and the time-wasting element of many TV programmes that have nothing to offer that is of educational or cultural value. Post-modernists, of course, would jump on the latter point with the riposte that value is a "meaningless and indefinable" concept, and so should not be raised in the first place. But as noted above, we repudiate the relativism of post-modernism as mischievous in undermining every aspect of rationality. The controversy is perhaps best settled through the understanding that as the new middle majority gains the full consciousness of its character and destiny, then ever-fewer numbers will be attracted to demeaning forms of populism, and that in the meantime it is better to let things take their natural course.

There is one aspect of populism, however, that should not be tolerated to take its natural course, and that is in regard to safeguarding public health. Britain is now in the leadership amongst the advanced industrial economies with her obesity crisis, and this is ruthlessly promoted by the giant corporations producing packaged and processed foods. Research has definitively demonstrated that the problem affects those at the base of society in all parts of the country. Excess sugar, salt and carbohydrates, in a wide range of foods are leading to obesity with its accompanying threats to the life of the less privileged, through diabetes, high blood pressure, heart disease, and cancer.

Whilst the government is shamefully confining itself to limited measures in fighting the social evil, for fear of upsetting the popular Household names, certain sections of the media, to its credit, have taken up the cudgel with crusading enthusiasm. This is a justifiable example, therefore, where the imposition of the knowledgeable may be exerted in influencing the free choice and attitudes of those at the base of society in safeguarding their welfare. As the costs of obesity put a heavy expenditure on the NHS that is another reason why the more discerning have a vested interest in reducing taxation arising through the self-imposed sickness of a poor diet.

So-called positive discrimination should be included as an integral part of the cult of proletarianisation. This is because, in its intentional discrimination between class differences, it chooses to lower standards in imposing a handicap against the better educated. This assumes that the proletarian is incapable of keeping abreast with standards decided by the authorities, and this results in three disadvantageous outcomes: firstly, the general dumbing down of educational standards; secondly, a process that demeans and/or oppresses standards that might have been expected from working class people; and thirdly, a bar in rationing the numbers of middle class students that might be accepted into desired courses. Whilst the third point is clearly a question of injustice, points one and two led the Labour government from 1997 onwards to trash the entire educational system from nursery to university levels, after a misleading campaign with the slogan, "Education, education, education!"

A just and proper resolution of the problem of education in creating a truly egalitarian society, is not to discriminate against chosen population sectors, but to establish a universal system of education on the assumption that all are equal, as found amongst any countries of North West Continental Europe. And where inequality or undesirable differences are identified then those should be boldly addressed by teachers in league with parents as described above.

Something must be added in regard to racial attitudes that are integral to the question of egalitarianism. The common approach until recently has been the call for multi-culturalism, but this is not a satisfactory answer to the problem, and indeed, may exacerbate the situation. Resolving racial prejudice, or raising the status of minorities to equality with the host population can only be achieved through national-culturalism, so that the former are integrated and fully accepted within the nation state. In this way, all essential differences are eliminated. Multi-culturalism, on the other hand, does no more than lock minorities into their original cultures, and so gives rise to every form of prejudice and discrimination.

New arrivals, therefore, should be given the opportunity to share and participate in every aspect of their adopted country. The above observations particularly apply to those of African descent or those from the Indian sub-continent or the Middle East. It may be argued that there is nothing more shocking than reminding the former of their slave origins (under the pretence of education) for that gives rise to embarrassment and awkwardness amongst those who have chosen their new homeland. If the question of slavery needs to be broached, it would be preferable to emphasise the fact that Britain was in the forefront for its abolition and fought courageously for a more humane world.

With regard to the Confucian peoples of the Far East, i.e., China, Korea and Japan, it may be said that in the present age, no such racial issues any longer exist. There are two reasons for this: firstly, the high level of their original civilisations in terms of both technology and the arts; and secondly, and most significantly, because technologically they may overtake the West in the very near future. The Confucian peoples have a quiet self-confidence in the superiority of their own cultures, and at the present time are hardly likely to take offence at any foolish gestures by ignorant persons to diminish their rightful status.

With the emergence of the Middle Majority, it would be the logical conclusion (as noted above) to model egalitarianism according to the values of that new majority. But the Cultural Marxists, who dominate intellectual thinking at the present time, fear that such a stance would culminate in enhancing the old middle class values, even though we have argued strongly for their repudiation. And in any case, such values are fast evaporating like frost on a sunny morn.

The Cultural Marxists could, of course, give a Marxist interpretation to the emergence of this new majority, as being itself the new "proletariat," and then all would be settled without further dispute. As the transformation of society over the past 100 years has taken so many twists and turns against the anticipated predictions of Marx, I would have thought that such a suggestion was not entirely unacceptable. On this note I leave readers to ponder on the above before drawing their own conclusions.

CHAPTER 3
The Socio-Economic Crisis of our Time

"Bankers had created a gambling culture in which the moral
borders between legitimate trading activity, recklessness
and criminal activity became ever more fuzzy – and the
disproportionate rewards disconnected from any economic
and social reality."

Will Hutton, *Them and Us: Changing Britain – Why we
Need a Fair Society*, Little Brown, 2010, p. 7.

We have shown above how the present system of
democratic government based on the left/right
conflict has become exhausted, or reached the end
of the line, or is no longer capable of serving as a medium
towards further progress. We have shown that it has reached
this impasse not through any internal failure but through its
considerable success.

In the advanced industrial economies, we are thankful for
all the benefits that democracy has brought over the past 60
years: an unprecedented raising of living standards; an
invaluable National Health Service without which existence
would be unthinkable; welfare benefits covering most
eventualities – despite severe cuts; and an outward sense of
security that never existed before in history. And yet all is not
well. Huge black storm clouds advance from the horizon. But
these are new problems, not recognised by our political
masters, or at least not comprehended within the remit of their
ideological understanding. They are problems that do not fit
within the parameters of the left/right conflict, and so are not
easily formulated on a theoretical basis for presentation to the
public as knockabout issues.

We are not talking here about climate change or environmental questions, which could easily be handled and agreed upon by all parties if they had the will, but socio-economic problems stemming from the heart of the financial-industrial system. These are matters that traditionally divide easily for a convenient punch-up between the left and right, but in this instance, leave both sides equally perplexed in silent stupefaction. The City and international financial institutions have always been inscrutable, but it is unusual for those on the right to not come forward with some kind of explanation in times of anxiety. The reason for the political embarrassment – for it is nothing less than this – is that the cause of the problem is not to be found in the text book of established or neoclassical economics, although we shall reveal below with clarity the simple cause of the problem.

The approaching storm clouds on the horizon comprise the accumulation of debt on debt, and it is astonishing that since the Banking debt crisis of 2008, and despite conferences and extensive research since then, that so little has been revealed for public exposure or discussion. Is it that the truth is too unspeakable to be revealed? The most immediate economic pressures in the public field stem from the hyper-inflation of property values – not merely of housing, but of land in both urban and rural areas. This has created a huge generational divide between the relative affluence of the older generation, and the prospective poverty of their children and grandchildren who may never afford to get their foot on the bottom rung of the property ladder. It may be asked, why did hyper-inflation hit the property market, whilst lesser rates hit other categories of goods?

If deprivation in the hope of a home was not bad enough, the younger generation have been hit by the double whammy of fast accelerating student loans which they may never be able to repay. The assurance that this need not be a threat unless earnings reach a certain level is little consolation, as decent employment prospects are few, and many highly skilled and expensively educated students find themselves stocking supermarket shelves for they know not how long.

Only now are the younger generation beginning to respond to their economic plight. After two decades or so of having withdrawn from party activity, they are now attaching themselves to Corbynism as a new hope for the future. Irrespective of the views one may have of Jeremy Corbyn's opinions, he is an original, consistent and honest politician, and a natural rebel within the Labour party establishment, and it is in these qualities that are found his fresh attraction amongst the young. But it should not be assumed that in embracing Corbynism they are also endorsing the ideology of the party.

As Ryan Shorthouse, the head of the Liberal Conservative think tank *Bright Blue*, has observed in an interview with the journalist, George Eaton, "It's a cultural problem that young people have with the Tories, not an economic problem with capitalism. If you look at most social attitudes surveys, there isn't a clamour for socialism among the young, they're quite sceptical of state welfare, they're very entrepreneurial. They believe heavily in individual and personal responsibility." ("People's Republic of London," *New Statesman*, 27th April 2018.)

This is in alignment with the tendencies we have described of the emerging 90% new majority, but of course it does not predict the direction in which any sector of the population may finally cast its vote. Whilst Jeremy Corbyn's refreshing radicalism may appeal to the young, the attractions of proletarianism plays no part in the situation. As long as he refers to the "many" he implies a recognition of the emergence of the new majority, and in so doing, he will hold the sympathy of his followers, but if he were to lapse into the careless use of such terms as the "proletariat" or the "working class," he would risk losing the vote of millions.

Meanwhile, those who have worked all their lives and retire to draw their pensions, discover to their horror that the Personal Pension schemes to which they signed up and had contributed for 30 or 40 years were based on a scam. The computer-generated estimates they were so enthusiastically shown by slick salesmen, were of course based on the optimistic predictions of equities, and no mention was made of their probable deflation. Consequently, retirement plans need to be cut back, and living standards are drastically reduced – often to survival level.

The Intergenerational Commission of the Resolution Foundation, a think-tank chaired by Lord Willetts, the former Tory Universities Minister, is currently addressing the above issues by calling for a £2.3 bn. NHS levy and a Citizen's Inheritance of £10,000 to be paid to the over 25s in an attempt to resolve the economic generational divide that will become increasingly intense in the near future. Such a gesture to alleviate the problem will, at best, merely touch at the margins of the situation, and only act as a temporary measure. This is because it only amounts to taking resources away from one financially oppressed sector and granting it to another. What is really needed to be effective is the root and branch radical reform of our financial institutions, as described in the following chapters of this book.

All the above situations transcend a class-based interpretation as they equally effect those across the entire spectrum of society, excepting the 2 ½% at the apex of the community. It might be thought that the left would exploit such a golden opportunity, but they don't. Firstly, in having turned their backs on the machinations of the business world, they are stunned with incomprehension by a self-imposed economic ignorance. Secondly, they have little interest in harnessing their cause to a supposedly one-time affluent middle majority for their concern is with an identifiable "Working class."

Thirdly, they have little sympathy with the idea of personally held property. Ideally, property should be "Collective," and as for homes, these should be sought through Council Housing. Those who involve themselves in unaffordable purchases should be left to stew in their own juice. And as for Personal Pension Plans, they were known to be a swindle all along, and so the ordinary man or woman should remain content with his State pension with perhaps the addition of SERPS. Such is the dismissive response of the left.

But far worse has occurred than those situations cited above. Personal debt per person in the UK has now reached an average of £8,000. A recent survey of Compare the market.com has revealed that 6 m. Britons fear never being debt-free; 25% are struggling to make ends meet; and 62% live in constant anxiety about their personal debt levels. The above figures are for mid-2018. Household debt is nearly £1.9 bn., or £300 m. higher than in 2007, and has increased by 7% in the 5 years up to 2017, whilst the household savings rate dropped below 5% in 2017, i.e., its lowest level since records began in 1963. Consumer and student debt have seen the greatest increases since 2012, rising from £1,518.5 bn. To £1,630.1 bn. In 2017.

Meanwhile, unsecured consumer credit has risen 19% in the past 5 years, mostly through credit cards, store cards, loans and overdrafts. It may also be noted that student debt has doubled in the past 5 years to £100.5 bn., whilst Council Tax arrears have increased by 12% in the same period. According to the Office of National Statistics, real average earnings in the UK have dropped 5% between 2008-2018, a stagnation of incomes in real terms not seen since detailed records began.

Most shocking of all, children in poverty has increased by 1 m. in the last decade. Looking at the global situation, although the world economy's real output is 25% greater than in 2007, the debt level has vastly increased, and is now 320% of global GDP, or 42% points more than in 2007, which historically is an unprecedented level.

In view of the above, the threat of living standards collapsing dramatically to those of a Third world country in the southern hemisphere have never been so real. Unless radical measures are taken, the bubble will sometime burst, and when such disasters occur, they come as sudden, unexpected and overnight events that strike equally at all, as none are prepared. Such was the situation in 1929 and 2008, and those closest to the world of finance contend that it is not a question of *if* but *when*.

The evidence for the future catastrophe and the reason for its cause should be obvious to every man and woman – and teenager, living in the advanced industrial economies. Pick up any household or other object and see where it is made. Imported products should not (and need not) be an economic burden, but due to the huge and accelerating imbalance of trade over the past decades, every finished imported product has become a millstone of debt around the neck of every living being. In their ignorance, our established parliamentary politicians, irrespective of party, will always spout the same stock reply in complacently explaining the situation: viz., that this is the inescapable consequence of "free" market forces in a global economy when cheaper sources of production are available elsewhere.

This smug reply is intended to kill off any further discussion in responding to the crisis, but it is made in ignorance of more significant factors concerning the nature of our financial-industrial system. It is a reply that will only satisfy those ideologically committed to the unreformed capitalist system as now lived on a day-to-day basis – and because they have turned their backs on the world of business, the left are as equally to blame as those on the far right. The economic problem of the present time did not merely begin with the imbalance of trade and imports from the Far East. Its origins have little to do with international trade of any kind.

The problem is traceable to grave faults in the financial-industrial system and even to the rationale or reason for conducting business enterprise. The decline of British industry is not traceable to the Post-War period or 1950, but rather to 1870, or even to 1851 with the hubris stemming from the Great Exhibition of that year, and the nemesis that followed. Likewise, how was it that the USA, the great victor of the Second World War, so quickly fell into industrial decline when all factors were in her favour?

The devastation of Detroit and other similar cities cannot be blamed on those who were defeated in the great conflict. Whilst our politicians, academics and financiers flounder around in incomprehension as to how the great problem of our time may be resolved, the most powerful and ridiculed leader of the day may yet emerge as the Shakespearian "fool" and the wisest man in the drama. The man who dances around the bankers with an accusing finger and cries, "America first," may have struck upon a point that needs further elaboration.

On more closely observing the successful and unsuccessful economies of the Post-War period, a clear pattern emerges. If the North West European Continental countries, together with the Far East Tigers, may be identified as the successful economies, on the grounds of their manufacturing and exporting record and the relatively higher growth of the living standards of their peoples; then America and Britain may be cited as the leading failing economies, on the grounds of their industrial decline and un-competitiveness in foreign markets, and their relatively sluggish improvement of living standards. The uninformed and superficial explanation of those committed to retaining the status quo in explaining the above situation, is that such success was simply due to the harder effort of their workers, whilst failure was due to the lack of motivation and constant strikes.

The real explanation, however, is that two quite separate systems of capitalism emerged. Firstly, we shall describe the systems and how they operate, and then we shall trace the different historical circumstances in which each developed. I was the first to differentiate between the Productive capitalism of the successful economies, and the Rentier capitalism of the failing economies in a pamphlet, *New Life for British Industry*, first published in 1985, financed by the prominent industrialist, George Goyder, and at that time widely read in SDP circles. Six years later the eminent French economist and financier, Michel Albert, published his book, *Capitalisme contre Capitalisme*, in Paris, in which he presented the same argument but using the terms, Rhine mode of capitalism, to include the Far East Tigers, and Neo-American capitalism, to describe the failing system.

The rationale of Productive capitalism is the maximisation of commercially viable market share in benefiting consumers, and the re-investment of sufficient profits to ensure the incorporation of the latest technology and most modern methods. Funding is primarily through the deficit financing of industrial investment credit banks with the in-depth knowledge of manufacturing to monitor commercial success. Hence bank directors are placed on the boards of companies to fulfil the similar role of management accountants as found in Anglo-Saxon enterprises. The advantage of the Bank Director is that he holds the possibility of offering unlimited loans in the right circumstances for company expansion or improvement, whilst the Management Accountant is usually limited to managing internal resources, so that repairs are preferred to the greater costs of replacement.

The management of the Productive company is intensely rational in its concentration on the product or service it provides, and these characteristics are furthered by the pressures of the bank in whose pocket they exist. In such a business environment there is little room for the attractions of the butterfly approach of diversification when severe competition or other difficulties loom. Equity or share-ownership options naturally occur in the larger scale enterprises. On the macro-economic level, Productive economies invariably experience higher relative living standards due to greater overall economic success and greater consumerism free of debt.

The rationale of Rentier capitalism is the maximisation of shareholders' profits. Whilst in Britain the purpose is more discreetly publicised, in America it is boldly proclaimed with pride through a plaque in the company foyer announcing its purpose. The rationale influences the entire character and mode of company operation. The maximisation of shareholders' profits may be undertaken by any legal means, but it primarily entails holding back on replacement or repairs; using the cheapest mode of factory construction (Continental visitors are appalled by the shoddiness of American industrial units); raising prices rather than increasing turnover for profitability; assuming a pretentiously high quality level to an inferior product for a better price; and reducing the quality or size of a product to retain a stable price.

The greatest ill of Rentier capitalism has occurred through conglomerate enterprise and its complex connection with stock exchange activity and international markets with their safe haven centres. Conglomerates are corporations owning a vast variety of diverse enterprises, most of which are bought up over a period of time in differing circumstances. Conglomerates exert an absolute financial control over their constituent parts which are otherwise supposedly autonomous, but they are held and used like cards in a poker pack.

Conglomerates accumulate enterprises for a variety of reasons, but it is rarely, if ever, because they "love" the particular industry or product entailed. Enterprises are accrued so that they may be asset-stripped and sold for the value of their land or buildings; or for short-term profitability before re-sale; or for transfer to an overseas territory; or for a longer-term purpose; or for stripping out and replacing the entire management, etc. The conglomerate has no more sensitivity for the feelings of those managing its subordinates than the unconscious cruelty of the auctioneer who sells off a herd of cows by the head to a crowd of waiting farmers.

There is inevitably a tension between the management of the subordinate enterprise and the interests of the corporate office. If the chief executive officer of the subordinate has not been bought off with a golden handshake and replaced by an accountant from the head office (which is most common), he and his team will attempt to retain the long-term interests of the enterprise as a first priority. This entails maximising market share, retaining stability, cultivating customer satisfaction, and anticipating developments for the future. The interests of the corporate office, on the contrary, are short-term. This means the maximisation of profits as soon as they may be made. If the speed of profitability of a particular enterprise is sluggish, then the head office will become impatient in calling either for its re-sale or asset-stripping.

And this brings into view another aspect of conglomerate business. Enterprises accumulate profits at very different speeds, not usually according to internal efficiency but according to type. A simpler business, such as a retailer with fast-moving products at a high value will often generate healthy profits over a short period of time; but a technologically complex business may be slow to generate profits because of reinvestment needs for machinery, etc. Such a standard for measuring profits naturally has nothing whatsoever to do with efficiency or good or bad management, but rather with the state of things at a particular point in time, but such a standard of measurement is of no interest to the conglomerate organisation.

Consequently, it is in this scenario that manufacturing in the Rentier economies in the Post-War period has encountered devastating disaster. Manufacturing has been discriminated against simply because it was manufacturing, and its ultimate proprietors refused to accept the time reality of the situation. Every business should be managed for its own best interests as defined by its purpose, and not to satisfy the threatening vested interests of any external body.

And yet that is exactly what conglomerate control entails. In the cause of justice and common sense, conglomerates should have no right to exist, since their only purpose is to benefit stockholders through sacrificing every proper purpose of the business enterprise.

CHAPTER 4
The Real cause of De-Industrialisation

"Nations fail today because their extractive economic
institutions do not create the incentives needed for people
to save, invest and innovate."

Daron Acemoglu & James A. Robinson, *Why Nations Fail*,
Profile Books, 2013, p. 372.

The maximisation of Rentier profits, or the making of
money out of money extends, of course, well beyond the
activities of the corporate organisation. It is the drive
behind every individual investor in the Rentier economy. Every
investor is entitled to the justifiable returns or interest from his
investments, but when such interest is excessive, or an
extortionate charge is placed on loans then that is usury defined
in the modern sense.

It is impossible to define the limit where justifiable
interest ends and usury begins, as so many imponderables are
involved, but it is always evident in assessing particular
situations. No advanced industrial economy can exist without
the charging of interest, but the Productive economies are free
of usury and free of the menace of usurers – or almost.

It is difficult for people in America or Britain to
comprehend the meaning of a usury-free society, and I shall
illustrate this by citing personal examples I encountered in
West Germany. Whilst working in that country at the start of
the 1960s, on a number of occasions I was confronted by fellow
Englishmen who confidently predicted the imminent demise of
the German economy. "This country is destined for bankruptcy
this year or next," went the argument. "These people can't
continue to borrow like they do – it's just crazy. Everyone in

this country can afford a new car. In Britain it would bankrupt the country." Predictions for the future of industry were even more dire. "Business is too ambitious here," it was insisted. "Soon industry will be insolvent and Britain will take the lion's share." It goes without saying that it was British industry which went insolvent, whilst German business continued to race ahead with unprecedented success.

Despite these early predictions, during the following decades, the British media and leading economists continued to downplay the German economy with depressing reports on declining living standards and poor industrial performance. During the same period, I visited the country on many occasions, sometimes for extended visits, both socially and on business. On each occasion I was astonished by the constant rise of living standards, the self-assurance of the people, and industrial success in all sectors of business. What, then, is the explanation for these grossly contradictory impressions? It is only to be found in the ignorance of commentators on how the German economy worked. They were clearly interpreting statistical data from a British viewpoint as to how the British financial-industrial system operated.

They were ignorant of Germany's investing and loan systems, and totally ignorant of the differences between Rentier and Productive capitalism. Such were the so-called "experts" overseeing the British economy! As the authors of *The Econocracy* have written in criticising established economics and its teaching, "Tomorrow's experts are being taught only one perspective as if there were no other way of doing economics. Critical and independent thinking is disadvantaged and there is little or no history, ethics or politics in economics courses." (Joe Earle, Cahal Maran & Zach Ward-Perkins, *The Econocracy, the perils of leaving economics to the experts*, Manchester University Press, 2017, p. 37) The trouble with commentators is that they assess the economy purely from the vantage point of the City's success, and in this they are led widely astray from an objective perspective. They seem totally incapable of discriminating between the falsities of the *phony* economy and the truths of the *real* economy.

When manufacturing declines, or has almost reached a state of collapse, or when the economy stagnates, as we have recently experienced, then investors seek out easier territories where profits may be made. Their last resort is found in the passive assets of land or property, as these entail no complex efforts in the generation of wealth. They just sit idly by and gather value through time.

Consequently, it is no surprise that over the past few decades there has been an accelerated rush by the super-rich and institutions to buy up property and land in both urban and rural areas. The inevitable result of this has been to push up values, and hence the hyper-inflation of housing costs as well as that of business premises and agricultural land. This is one of the greatest socio-economic evils of our time for it is a process that destroys Creative Wealth. And here we must discriminate between benign *Productive Wealth Creation* and self-destructive *Rentier Wealth Creation*. Productive profitability defines the margin of justifiable interest rates; whilst Rentier profitability crosses the margin into the area of extortionate interest rates and usury. In this context it may be noted that in 2017 financial sector bonuses alone paid out by the City of London amounted to £152 bn.

The most dramatic example of the widespread self-destructiveness of Rentier profitability may be witnessed through the events of the Thatcher-Reaganite era. In the words of Anthony Sampson, "During 1980, when factories were closing down and businesses going bankrupt, the British banks were declaring record profits. It looked like a return to a pre-industrial economy, dominated by money-lenders." (*The Money Lenders*, Hodder & Stoughton, 1981, p. 205.) It was not foreign competition that destroyed industry in the Western world but the financial institutions that supposedly should have been reinvesting in the infrastructure of their countries. Hence money-makers were and are continuing to derive profits not from productivity but from de-industrialisation, and yet the political establishment and media remain silent on this destructive process.

And this brings into question the value of the super-rich who visit or settle in this country. It has always been assumed that the wealthy with their largesse should be welcomed into Britain in anticipation of their contribution to the economy. Great wealth, it is argued trickles downwards, in eventually benefitting even the poorest in the community. This may have been the situation 100 or more years ago when industrialists from France, Germany (e.g., Friedrich Engels), and elsewhere, settled in Manchester and other northern cities, and founded their factories employing thousands, but that is certainly not the situation today. We now experience the opposite movement of finance: that is the upward movement of prices.

The super-rich from many lands settle in Britain and not only pay extortionate prices for prime property, but in so doing set off a mechanism that raises the prices of all property reaching down to even homes and buildings in the poorest areas. Following on from this it may be noted that home ownership in the capital has fallen below 50% (compared to the UK average of 63.5%) being the lowest level since the early 1980s, and it is forecast to drop even further to 39.5% by 2025. The average house price in London is currently £471.986, compared to the UK average of £225,000, which amounts to 14 times the average London salary of £34,200. It may also be noted that the number of renters in London doubled to 21%

between 2001 and 2011, and that the typical private renter now spends 48% of their income on housing costs.

And not only does the presence of the super-rich inflate the values of property, for it also extends to a wide variety of goods and services, beginning in the capital and then spreading to other centres throughout the country. They certainly have the golden touch, but as with Midas, it is the touch of death, for the irrational inflation of monetary values leads to the gradual destitution of the ethnic population through unaffordability and debt. Hence the presence of the super-rich in our midst is not a credit but a heavy liability.

Associated with this problem, but more serious and on a larger scale, is the curse of undesirable inward investment in essential utilities and major service infrastructures as airports and docks. This, of course, stems from international free market forces which have dangerously usurped what formerly belonged to the public sector. The risks of surrendering such vital resources as electricity, gas and water – and most notably our railway system, to foreign control cannot be exaggerated, for we are thereby relinquishing our responsibility for national integrity, and in a conflict situation may encounter catastrophe. The price inflation of these utilities has risen out of all proportion to general prices since their foreign takeover. It is surprising that Japan already had the percipience to recognise the dire outcome of inward foreign investment exactly 150 years ago, whilst in Britain we have still not learned the lesson by 2018.

Having described how two systems of capitalism operate in different ways, we must now turn to their origins and history to explain how the economy stands at the present day. Rentier capitalism may be traced to a trading environment from the 16th century, especially through the events of English history. At that time England was amongst one of the later countries in

Western Europe to awaken to the promises of an imperial future. She was also one of the poorest countries amongst the larger nation states, and her population was relatively less than that of her neighbours. It should be remembered that when an approach was made to Henry VII to finance an expedition of Christopher Columbus to explore a shorter route to India across the Atlantic, he pleaded poverty and that his country was in no position to indulge in such hazardous adventures.

Within 50 years Spain had grabbed the greater part of the Americas and although she had occupied but a small part of the northern continent, she claimed the legal ownership of all. Furthermore, the right to this ownership was endorsed by the Vatican, whilst Brazil was meanwhile generously granted to Portugal. At that time Britain had nothing, and so on awakening to the worldwide commercial opportunities during the Elizabethan age, she was already placed in a disadvantageous situation. England's response was not motivated so much by a desire for imperial glory, as by a defensive stance in maintaining a balance of power with her European neighbours – a policy she has maintained until the present day. Whilst trading companies were established in different parts of the Eastern world, the main attraction of the Americas were the huge deposits of gold and silver supposedly available from diverse peoples and all kinds of hidden resources in a jungle environment.

What followed was an era of difficult trading and widespread piracy. A blind eye was turned to the latter by the authorities and later by its semi-official recognition. The risks of investors in such a trading environment were high: shipwreck, disease amongst crews, the capture or destruction of English vessels by enemy states, or the breakdown of trading relationships with princes in the Indian sub-continent. This necessitated that high returns should be paid to investors if business development was to flourish. The conflict with Spain has always been portrayed in the Northern hemisphere as a purely religious struggle, but in fairness to a former enemy, it is far more probable that the Armada raised against England in 1588 was driven more by the threat of piracy rather than concern over religious scruples.

Britain's great era of financial-commercial re-organisation, that established foundations for imperial pre-eminence, followed the Glorious Revolution of 1688-89, with the adoption of Dutch investing practices and the establishment of the Bank of England in 1694. The outcome of the 7 years' war (in reality the first world war) in 1756-1763 ensured Britain's place as the world's leading economy and imperial power for almost 200 years, and although the City of London should be given credit for achieving this success until the middle of the 18th century, it should be borne in mind that Britain was predominantly a trading rather than a manufacturing nation.

The Industrial Revolution created a new scenario in which the City played a negligible role in its early history. It was the personal savings of a large wealthy class, and later, the investments of innumerable provincial banks that launched modernisation and mass production. Throughout the 19th century the provincial banks that had taken on untested practices and high risks, often fell into foolish or even criminal situations, giving rise to frequent scandals, and by the end of the century, through absorption or bankruptcy, the 300 or so banks were reduced to several dozen. Nonetheless, manufacturing industry continued to expand at an unprecedented rate in eventually dominating the markets of the world.

It was not until towards the close of the 19th century that industrial corporate structures began to take their modern form, at first through shipbuilding, the railways, major civil engineering projects, and heavy chemicals, and later auto manufacturing; and at a much later date, the formation of conglomerates with their many and diverse enterprises. It should also be borne in mind that City institutions, and all those forms of business drawn into stock market activity, charged higher rates of interest and paid out better dividends, than equivalent institutions in Continental Europe or the Far East due to historical circumstances as explained above.

We must now turn to the history of Productive capitalism before describing the interrelationship of the two, leading eventually to the contemporary situation. Britain's domination of so many products in the world market could not last forever amongst other otherwise advanced European nations and those further afield. The imbalance of trade brought to importing nations was bound sometime to be recognised as an intolerable burden. Whilst in Britain the free trade laissez-faire philosophy of Adam Smith prevailed, this was contradicted in Germany and elsewhere with the protectionism of Friedrich List. The need to confront the competitiveness of British power was not merely an option but a question of survival. But how? One could call on the traditional mercantilism of the past but that was not sufficient in itself in the modern age.

In the closing decades of the 19th century, or from the 1850s onwards, one might call on the family wealth of the affluent to generate industrial resurgence but that too was impractical. It was no longer the 18th century for in the meantime technology had become too costly to depend on privately owned resources. The answer could only be found in a solution that would horrify anyone committed to promoting the British business culture.

It was the power of the state that needed to resolve the situation. Consequently, not only was there a need to establish specialised industrial investment credit banks to lend long term at low rates of interest, but to establish business, technical, and engineering colleges in professionalising all aspects of commercial life, and furthermore, to establish a close cooperation between the state and business, in addition to cleverly planned import controls that were sufficiently covert to avoid the ire of other nation states. All this resulted in creating a very different business culture: more intense and serious in contrast to the playful optimism and more relaxed quick-footed willingness to diversify in the face of painful competition as found in Britain. On the Continent business was not perceived as a "game," but as a deadly struggle for survival.

The most remarkable story of industrial resurgence was that of Meiji Japan, which over a 30-year period from 1868 jumped from a 17th century technology to a modern state on an equal level with any Western economy. Her leaders not only had the courage to resist the naval armaments of the USA, but the presence of mind to resist the greater threat of incoming foreign investment. In safeguarding national integrity, the strengthened Imperial government had the wisdom to apply the so-called policy of "Restoration," entailing the surrender of the fixed stipends paid to the 1.9 million aristocratic Samurai class to the state to "promote civilisation and enlightenment through modern ethics and ideas."

Whilst in 1868 the Meiji emperor announced in his Charter Oath that "knowledge shall be sought all over the world in thereby strengthening imperial rule," in 1873 under the leadership of Mori Arinori, a group of Japanese intellectuals were formed under the title of the Meiji Six Society, and they put into place the practical measures for the transformation of their country. Japan could never have eventually become the great power that she did in the 20th century if she had not pursued her own interests so single-mindedly whilst resisting the damaging economic aspects of internationalism that would have compromised the best interests of her majority. Her success is all the more surprising in view of the poverty of her natural resources, and her geographical isolation as an island people at the far end of the world. In the want of any other explanation, her success can only be attributed to the natural genius of her people and that of her leaders.

It was only in the Post-War period that a sharp contrast became apparent between the Productive and Rentier economies, and the astonishment that struck leading thinkers as to why the successful economies were successful and the failing economies unsuccessful. Why should the victors in the Second World War prove so dismally industrially in time of peace, whilst the defeated (especially) thrived victoriously? For decades, all the wrong answers were suggested, viz., that the morale of the defeated was boosted by the realisation that they could sink no lower into the depths, whilst the victors were left exhausted and demoralised by their struggle and foolishly anticipated immediate material rewards for their patriotic efforts in war. Strikes and industrial conflict achieved nothing in stemming decline.

Most surprising was the fact that the emergence of two quite separate systems of capitalism was not even recognised by thoughtful commentators until well after the damage had been done. Hence no intelligent discussion arose in industrial, political, or academic circles. The main reason for this may well have been the convictions of ideology during the Cold War period, viz., the fixation that there only existed two forms of industrial organisation: the Capitalist, that must be defended at any cost, and the Communist, that must be fought off by any means. Strong convictions in the face of danger often have a tendency to kill off intelligent speculation and generate stupidity, but this was further advanced by the idea of the perfectibility of the existing capitalist system, and that its leading doctrines should remain unchanged and unquestioned as a safeguard against the horrors of possible heresy – i.e., in adopting the alternative strategies of West Germany or Japan.

America was clearly in the forefront of this struggle in defending what became known as the free market forces of Neo-liberalism, and from the 1980s onwards, measures were taken to strengthen the ideology and its practices through the policy of extending de-regulation. When the suspicion arose that there existed an alternative form of capitalism, this was angrily repudiated as not being in any sense a "proper" capitalism – and this response was accepted without question or any attempt to examine the facts of the overall situation. The far right, therefore, adopted an attitude that was almost identical with that of the far left: viz., that capitalism was capitalism as an inescapably unitary system that could not be divided into separate types. This not only placed an intellectual block on the analysis of reality but enforced stupidity on those who adopted such an attitude.

If Productive capitalism was so much more successful than its Rentier counterpart, in both production and in serving the broader social interests of the majority, then why has it not triumphed as a worldwide system? Apart from the obvious fact that history does not always ensure the wisest decision-making, there are several circumstances that need to be considered. Firstly, the Anglo-American powers led the world against the threat from the East, and so the thinking and policies of these leading nations were accepted by their friendly neighbours as standing on firm foundations.

Secondly, the American brand of Rentier capitalism predominated over that of any other territory – including Britain. During the Thatcher-Reaganite era, it was the penetration of American systems and new types of financial services, together with advancing de-regulation, that were to overwhelm Britain. Michel Albert's book, *Capitalism Against Capitalism*, was published in Paris in 1991, as a warning to the Continental peoples against the advance of Rentier capitalism – for Britain was to be used as a launching pad for the advance of American financial power. But Albert's book appeared too late to stem the threat. From the 90s onwards, American financial thinking and practices began to penetrate the European Continent, amongst other peoples, and most notably the Far East Tigers. Japan was already in deep trouble by the early 1990s with the collapse of investment values and a decline in productivity, and difficulties soon followed in other significant economies as Thailand and Malaysia.

Thirdly, the economic might of China soon made its impact felt throughout the advanced economies of the Western world. That, in conjunction with the new American influence, soon awoke leading business people to the attractions of the Rentier approach. With downsizing and offshoring, or the transfer of manufacturing to distant overseas locations, financiers everywhere sought a new approach to money-making, not willingly out of casual choice but for the survival of their livelihoods.

Although this did not entail the immediate downfall of Productive capitalism, new business values were widely adopted following the determination of American systems to prevail over earlier practices. Consequently, by the start of the 21st century, such countries as Germany and the Scandinavian states were still relatively more productive than Britain or America although serious inroads had meanwhile been made to undermine their productive base.

Today there is a confusion of values in Continental Europe as well as in the Far East. This is not to suggest that Rentier capitalism is still happily accepted in either Britain or the USA.

Everywhere disillusion has crept in. Even in America the great dream is beginning to vanish, and the shock of this is leading to chaos and the angry rejection of both mainstream parties as they have traditionally existed. What does the future hold, and how can Productive capitalism be regenerated to serve majority populations throughout the world?

A first step might be to argue the essential need for discriminating between political and financial power, or the constitutional requirement for government to exert political authority which is free from financial vested interests. If government is to be sufficiently objective in avoiding entanglement either pro or contra in regard to financial interests, and if it is to be truly free of corruption or undesirable cupidity of any kind, then special measures should be taken in the choice of our representatives. Whilst on the one hand our representatives should be knowledgeable in the many aspects of business, and warned against its serpentine methods in influencing public administration; on the other hand, they should be forbidden to hold directorships or shares in any kind of enterprise.

The existing regulations in enforcing a declaration of business interests, is clearly insufficient in preventing corruption or the wholesale takeover of party political systems by powerful corporations and their interests. It may be suggested that it is almost impossible for our representatives to be knowledgeable of business without internal involvement in its practice. In response to such a situation the following measures are proposed: firstly, that all elected representatives should surrender directorships and the ownership of company shares, but receive compensatory payments in lieu of this; secondly, that those without business experience should undergo an appropriate course on the open and covert political influence of business; and thirdly, that all those standing for election should take an oath swearing that they will not be swayed by gifts, endowments, or other inducements by commercial or other organisations or individuals of any kind.

The above conditions should not only be imposed on elected representatives but also on all levels of those employed by the Civil Service, and in addition, that no Civil Servant on retirement from the service should at any time be allowed to be employed by a corporation or financial institution. The guidance or overriding principle in defining the above should be the underlying influence of Productive over Rentier transactions. I cannot envisage that any lesser measures would be sufficient in promoting the better interests of majorities in nation states.

Before outlining the principles entailed in the Personalisation of Ownership, it would be useful to describe the desirable conditions in which business as a general activity should be encouraged to flourish amongst ordinary people. This will assist in allaying the irrational prejudices of those who are suspicious of, or who disdain business, for any reason whatsoever. That is, we should all have a positive idea of the framework within which business should ideally exist.

Business operates in many different ways in different cultures, and here we are concerned with its existence in the advanced industrial economies, where in any case it may better serve majority needs than in any other culture. As a general rule, business effecting the day-to-day lives of ordinary people has greater integrity according to the increased prosperity and stability of the nation state. Contrariwise, the poorer a society, the more difficult and dishonest are business practices for ordinary people to handle. The main reason for this is obvious: the greater the poverty the more difficult it is for business people to "turn an honest penny," and it may be said that the latter are forced into duplicity, not through the wish to deceive, but through inevitable circumstances in the fight for survival.

A secondary reason is that in such societies, established custom and law for a more proper conduct of business is not only unenforceable but the fact is unofficially recognised by the authorities with the consequence that a chaotic situation pertains. There are countries in both Africa and Asia (as well as elsewhere), for example, where if the West European were to be suddenly transferred on a magic carpet, he would not "last" for a day, so intolerable are the conditions for buying and selling. On buying a packet of rice he may find it one third filled with pebbles; a non-sealed cap on a bottle of "fresh water" may be a container with un-potable liquid (the author of this book was hospitalised for 5 days as the result of such in incident in Yemen); the first bite of food taken outside a 5-star hotel may lead to 24 hours of illness; and in purchasing any product or service, he may pay 100% more than any local would agree to.

The more advanced an economy, the more rational and complex tend to be the conditions for existence, with all kinds of rules and regulations in place to which ordinary people may be willing to refer. In developing or backward economies, on the other hand, there is greater informality, and where rules and regulations do exist, they are more easily waived. Business in any society, irrespective of the stage of development, is always based on trust, but again, the nature of trust in its limits or discretion is very variable in differing parts of the world. In all the above matters it is difficult to talk about the morality of a society when the struggle for survival needs to be prioritised in all decision-making.

In summary, it may be concluded that all those who live in the advanced industrial economies may be thankful for the rationality and rule of law that ensures a high level of predictability and morality in the conduct of business between ordinary people on the personal level. The nature of business on a higher level, in regard to corporations and financial institutions, belongs of course, to another sphere, and hence to a different level of discussion.

It may be noted that, as yet, no reference has been made in this book to the highly emotive and unresolvable concepts of the "EU" or "Brexit," and this may appear as all the more surprising in view of the fact that the leading arguments presented must have influenced the author in a certain direction. Any mention of the above concepts has been intentionally avoided as an unnecessary distraction from the far more important thesis presented in these pages. We are here making a comparison between economic circumstances that demonstrably benefit or dis-benefit majorities, as against the rule-breaking of regulatory procedures that have no proven value either way.

The underlying arguments of this book are of greater import and of longer term significance than any matters covering the discussion of Brexit. To have included the latter, with all its complexity and divisive questions, into the discussion of the socio-economic topics addressed in this book would only have caused confusion without throwing any new or useful light on the overall political situation. In complementing the above approach, it may be noted, there is no intention of criticising established parliamentary parties or their representatives *in themselves* in the trust they possibly accept the main conclusions of this book either openly or covertly.

CHAPTER 5
Achieving the Personalisation of Ownership

"What concerns me is the lack of serious public debate about
how globalisation and deliberate Government policy has
empowered those with particular financial talents to make
vast sums of money for themselves, while disempowering
the rest of us."

Robert Peston, *Who Runs Britain,?* Hodder & Stoughton,
2008, p. 27.

All political action begins with theory or a set of guiding
principles based on relevant knowledge for the way
ahead. When knowledge loses its credibility through
the misinterpretation of facts, or through a change of socio-
economic circumstances that undermine the validity of
accepted knowledge, as sometimes occurs during crucial points
in history, then uncertainty and chaos is the outcome. Such a
situation now confronts the peoples of the advanced industrial
economies, and if all the world is eventually to move ahead on
the same level of progress, then all humankind will be similarly
confronted.

If ideology is broadly defined as a system of belief, then
we live in an age when it is eschewed as touched by
superstition, and in its place we resort to pragmatism which is
a short-term approach to practical decision-making with the
solidity of its step-by-step assurance. But pragmatism, with its
shorter-term view, tends to compound rather than resolve
problems, although it does ideally serve the narrow interests of
the parliamentary politician with his eye on the next election.
The age of pragmatism has been marked by the poverty of
ideas, and one stupidity followed by another, as outdated and

futile ideological convictions are nonetheless unconvincingly maintained as a back-up and repeated in a parrot-like fashion.

The answer is not the consignment of ideology to extinction as a matter of principle, but the condemnation of old and discredited ideologies to allow in the development of new thought. The left/right conflict is not only bankrupt because as a democratic mechanism it no longer advances the cause of progress, but because each of its ideologies are no longer of value or utility in themselves.

Whilst the failure of socialism in any form as a practical or ethical system should have been recognised with the collapse of the Berlin Wall in 1989, so likewise the failure of Neo-liberalism or Rentier capitalism should be recognised with the banking debt crisis in 2008. The attempt to revive either of these two corpses is not only to defy practical common sense, but to defy morality. They are two false gods, dependent on one another, and in their interacting struggle, they worsen the longer-term interests of humankind.

We are here talking about values and the need to create a new ethical system to fit the transformation of society for the world of the future. A new ethical ideology is required to fulfil the needs of all humankind and not one half of the population against the other. A modern ethics needs to return to the inspiration of Greek thought whereby goodness is defined as striving towards quality in all its aspects, and in the belief that intelligence and knowledge is the key to discovering virtue and a better life. This means that intelligence and knowledge should be regarded as values in themselves, together with their facilitating origin and outcome, i.e., constructive curiosity and exploration. Such characteristics necessarily call for an individualistic upwardly aspirational society, or in a democratic environment, what we have described as aspirational egalitarianism.

Ethics based on such values may be interpreted as conflicting with those traditional and now outdated Christian values of viewing knowledge as "sin," and goodness as self-imposed poverty and the renunciation of all the material benefits and pleasures of life. It is important to raise these factors, for whilst they would not be openly assented to by any balanced person in the modern age, their unconscious influence on the attitudes of many is still of significance. Hence, whilst many left-leaning people may be afflicted irrationally with feelings of guilt at their own good fortune in a world where widespread misery still exists, they are seized by emotional ideas that are of little help in resolving major issues.

It is far better, then, to look at the broader picture of existence from a more disinterested viewpoint in designing more effective and longer term solutions in resolving the underlying crises of humankind and the environment. Those who are overwhelmingly oppressed by a sense of "sin," would therefore do better in seeking to remove it through psychological self-understanding, rather than luxuriating in its morbid satisfaction.

As demonstrated in the earlier chapters of this book, both socialism and neo-liberalism, seek only to fulfil the narrow interests of particular population sectors, although their proponents would argue otherwise. Whilst socialism can only feed on the motivation of resentment, and enmity towards business howsoever organised; neo-liberalism can only survive though the exploitation of usury which is ultimately self-destructive of productive business enterprise.

A fair society can only be based on aspirational egalitarianism, that equates with a nice balance between equality and freedom. And this is only achievable through the *Personalisation of Ownership*, and the latter is only practicable through the emergence of the New Majority in a fully developed democracy. The personalisation of ownership is to be contrasted sharply with Privatisation which is Newspeak for corporate control, and hence has nothing to do with anything properly described as "private;" as it is also to be contrasted with socialism's common ownership, that is no proper ownership as control is in the hands of external representative elites.

The personalisation of ownership, on the other hand, is linked essentially to the individual on a direct basis whenever practicable, as opposed to representative power that filters the will of the individual before reaching its end purpose. The conditions for the personalisation of ownership are dependent on the presence of an advanced industrial economy where the majority are highly informed and responsible as individuals for many aspects of their personal and occupational lives.

Such an individual does not regard him- or herself as a subject of the state but as an integral part of its existence, and hence is actually free of compulsion and not merely of the consciousness of compulsion. This is enabled through the widespread extension of rights in an open society – as already exists, for example, in Scandinavia and elsewhere. Such a society is classless in the sense of its unitary structure and conditions, and the necessary legal changes made to company law in regard to broadening ownership and control.

If the achievement of the above measures sound radical to the point of utopianism, it should be recognised that huge steps towards the extension of such freedom have already been taken over the last half century, and they are measures that would have been inconceivable 100 years earlier. The ownership of the means of production, distribution, and the means of exchange, may evoke images of a socialist-like society, but we are now driving towards something that is a very different scenario. The collectivism of socialism is designed for manipulating an uninformed and herd-like proletariat that is only intent on and accustomed to the shoulder-to-shoulder repetitive tasks of the conveyer belt. All trust is placed in the ideological declarations of a dictatorial elite in enforcing conformity.

In the realisation that modern modes of robotised manufacturing have very little resemblance to the industry of the past, we recognise that the highly trained skills of the workers of the future will put them on a similar educational level with scientists, doctors, lawyers, or accountants, etc., and with this, their status will be enhanced in an egalitarian environment. As the narrowing of margin levels between differing skills will bring top and lower employees to a closer relationship, this will inevitably erode tensions and improve understanding in all its aspects.

As with all occupational spheres, workers will need their trades unions in protecting their interests, but the factory workers' union of the future will rather have the characteristics of the General Medical Council than a strike-obsessed body intent on the "overthrow of capitalism." The transformation of the world of work will in itself be sufficient to ensure that such an organisation will put its emphasis on the professionalisation of skills rather than on the demand for rights. In such a society, mainstream rights will anyway have already been established.

Co-determination in the management of the enterprise will be linked to share ownership schemes, and the employee's level of investment in his concern would be decided by seniority and years of service. As we have seen with such success in West Germany and Japan in the Post-War period, a permanent and strong bond would be maintained with the state, in ensuring commercial viability and proper protective measures, and in the rare event of misadventure, or the collapse of the enterprise, the state would have in readiness other arrangements for employing the redundant – as already exists in Germany. Hence the employee's security would not only have the support of directors and senior management, in addition to personal commitment expressed through managerial and financial investment, but also the over-arching authority of the state ultimately responsible for national prosperity.

All these conditions would give positive assurance to directors leading the company. Personal or family ownership would be guaranteed to those in charge of small or medium-sized companies, providing they were competently run; and whilst with small companies of ten employees or less, such ownership would be absolute; with larger companies, on the demise of the proprietor, a vote of employee confidence may be taken in confirming the heir as the new chief executive officer.

The principle of passing on the inheritance of an enterprise is sound, as it helps maintain continuity and the confidence of stability in the minds of employees, although in the real world, due to a number of factors, inheritance rarely extends in a straight line beyond the third generation. Whilst the founder of an enterprise always occupies a unique situation, his heirs as CEOs are rather like constitutional monarchs in giving the enterprise a sense of tradition, and if not the assurance then at least the illusion of stability and the greater probability for a successful future.

Relationships between the different sectors committed to the enterprise, i.e., directors, managers, junior employees and investors, would be based on firmer and more amicable foundations in the future than hitherto, on a number of counts. Primarily, this would be manifested through a cultural environment of an aspirational egalitarian society, as described in these pages, that has never existed previously in the history of humankind. In the past authority has always been exerted by minority elites, irrespective of whether we consider military or religious monarchies, oligarchies of various kinds, or even democracies as they have existed until the present time. We are now describing the emergence of full democracy, comprising a kind of flattened authority, achieved through a sophisticated form of administration where power is balanced through its more equal and fairer distribution.

In such a society where it is difficult to envisage how further steps may be taken in adding to the sum total of fairness and justice, not only will a new psychological consciousness arise as to the natural struggle of life, but major branches of philosophy that have dominated thinking for 3,000 years will need to be reconsidered. This is because political philosophy has always defined society and the resolution of its problems from the perspective of class: e.g., in the ancient world, slaves, free citizens and foreigners; and in the modern world, the proletariat, bourgeoisie, and nobility. In societies where huge social divides have either been obliterated or reduced in intensity to a fraction of their former significance, there will inevitably be changes in human relationships. This may perhaps best be illustrated by citing the more impartial attitudes on ethical issues and the holding of emotion in check, as found amongst the democratic cultures of northern Continental Europe. In such advanced cultures, rationality strives to overcome the pull of passion.

The proprietors of enterprises where ownership and control is shared out amongst employees in such a milieu, would be free of anxiety as to any encroachment on their rightful authority, as the positive commitment of employees would be so extensive, and state protection so reassuring, in promoting the cause of productivity and balanced relationships. Compare this with a society where, in terms of the electorate, one half of the population is sympathetic to business, whilst the other half holds it in disdain as an unpleasant even if inescapable activity. A new moral ethic is necessary in uniting the population towards a positive attitude in pursuing business activity and this can only be achieved through aspirational egalitarianism.

Furthermore, it is necessary that the different sectors committed to the enterprise should view its purpose from a single perspective, so that vested interest issues are held in check and prevented from emerging as divisive factors. And that single purpose would be the concentration on *Productive profitability* in assessing sound business in all the departments of its activity. In every decision, there is a line defining the good of the business as a thing in itself, as opposed to that which is only of selfish benefit to specific sectors involved in its management. Of course, there cannot at all times be unanimity on what benefits the end purpose of the enterprise, and so this presents the opportunity for discussion. Rentier decision-making, or when the balance of outcome compromises the long-term prosperity of the company should always be criticised and condemned.

The blatant usurious practices of conglomerate management are clearly identifiable as detrimental, but there are innumerable other everyday decisions needing closer examination before action is taken. When should replacement have priority over repair?; When may salary increases be demonstrated as increasing productivity?; When may it be proven to boost profitability through product turnover by reducing unit prices?; How may working hours or heating adjustments be proven to increase working efficiency, etc.? The dialectic of Productive profitability is not dependent on subjective criteria but on a striving towards objective factors.

There can be no such thing as absolute objectivity, for opinion varies and reason is subject to relative considerations.

However, subjective or self-centred motives are usually recognisable, despite subtle attempts at disguise, and if Productive profitability is always upheld as the end purpose, then greater care will be taken in decision-making. The individual who is too often denounced for Rentier preferences will soon arouse the ire of colleagues, and unless he mends his ways, will eventually lose his place in the company.

Before parting from the topic of Productive profitability it is necessary to remark on several other aspects of the highly emotive subject of Profit. Left-leaning people have always tended to disdain profit, or even to condemn it outright with the explanation that production should be for *use* but not for *profit*. We accept that it should be for *use* in the sense of fulfilling desirable consumer needs, but in an exchange society, an attempt to outlaw the principle of profit is nonsense. Every commercial transaction is either made at a profit or loss, howsoever difficult it may be to judge one way or the other. Profit not only has many uses but may be interpreted in different ways in fulfilling varied purposes.

The main uses of profit are the following: for the payment of wages or the salaries of all those committed to the business; for re-investment for updating machinery and methods, etc.; for the payment of dividends to investors; and for fulfilling the taxation demands of the state. Different interpretations of profit are required for the following: for taxation purposes, taking into consideration legal tax avoidance (not to be confused with illegal tax evasion); the valuation of the company for sale to another party; advance estimates of profit for forward planning or expansion; the presentation of accounts to investors; estimates in view of a probable economic crisis; or, accounts for winding up the company in the event of insolvency.

All the above need to be taken in view of complex accountancy regulations and frequent changes in the law. The above is also a stark reminder that if business is to benefit the majority then it is necessarily dependent on a benevolent state in ensuring its success, not only through appropriate tax regulations, but in adjusting the exchange rate of the currency in aiding international competitiveness. The business lobby that cries constantly for independence from the state, or governments that advocate that "free markets" need to be free from state interference, are only supporting the Rentier capitalism that benefits the few. This is because Rentier capitalism is a self-enclosed system that operates separately from all external interests.

At the start of this book we noted that the existence of democracy can only be maintained through struggle on the interpretation of realistic economic concepts demanding resolution, and not merely through invented or artificial differences that are presented as a basis for conflict. The central thesis of this book is that the left/right struggle has lost its utility as a democratic medium in furthering progress, and hence the present crisis of democracy.

The crisis is already entailing the erosion of democratic government through the silent growth of bureaucracy; the seizure of unaccountable power by the financial-industrial system; the increasing apathy amongst the majority as to how we are governed; and the passive acceptance of "bread and circuses" as a satisfactory substitution for freedom and free institutions. It is in the light of these factors that we are now presenting the principle of Productive profitability as the only realistic dialectic for regenerating democracy in the future. It is a principle that strikes at the core of the greatest economic evil confronting the peoples of the world today, viz., the self-destructive forces of Rentier capitalism.

This calls for the re-organisation of business through the Personalisation of Ownership. This naturally entails promoting business on the smaller scale wherever this is practicable, for in so doing, business ownership is increased; the possibilities for innovation and desirable competition are extended; consumer choice is broadened; the power of monopolies is broken; and the financial hegemony of corporations is held in check. The maintenance of corporations will still be necessary for essentially large scale industry as auto manufacturing, shipbuilding, heavy chemicals, etc., although they will be transformed internally through democracy, and externally in their relationships through democratic accountability.

It is vital that employee share ownership and those others engaged in the direct management of the enterprise from the CEO downwards, should be differentiated from the share ownership of external investors. If such a distinction was not respected there might always exist the possibility of directors secretly conspiring with external investors for any nefarious purpose, e.g., for meddling with dividend policies for Rentier purposes, or conspiracies for moving the enterprise to a foreign location, or other policies that might compromise the cause of productivity. The first purpose of employee share ownership should be to unite the interests of all those directly involved in the management of the enterprise towards a single goal; and only secondarily for the purpose of personal profit. Both purposes naturally contribute to the cause of maintaining the independence of the enterprise against the intrusion of external interests. Whilst internal investors are therefore in a strict sense part-owners, external investors should only be held as wise risk-takers whose only interest is for their personal profit.

With regard to conglomerates, and their hundreds of diverse enterprises, they should be broken up and their constituent parts restored to independent status, via, if necessary, the assisting measures of industrial investment credit banks established for the purpose. If such proposals are embarked upon, the proprietors of the conglomerates would be justified in rising up in alarm as to what is intended for their future. These financiers, with their considerable knowledge of business in all its diversity, should be re-employed in the establishment of the new type of banks, as cited above, in participation with the assisting skills of leading advisers from Continental Europe and Japan.

For a variety of reasons, the reform of the financial-industrial system can only be undertaken through prioritising the national interests of each nation state. For a start, international or Global financial interests are in conflict with the national interests of majorities in that they are not democratically accountable to the nation state. Offshore tax havens need to be closed where they operate in small isolated locations for that purpose alone, as countries are thereby prevented from collecting the taxes that are rightfully due to them. There may be legal loopholes that seemingly justify such avoidance, but morally, no such justification may be upheld. With regard to centrally located places for laundered money, as London, New York, or Zürich, legislation should be enacted in protecting all nation states through international cooperation, and where criminality is identified this should be attended to as appropriate.

In the 21st century, perhaps the major argument for promoting national interests in the financial sphere is as an insurance policy against the prospects of global collapse. Every nation should take on the responsibility for maximising its own self-sufficiency, firstly with regard to feeding its own population, and secondly with manufacturing all its essential and other needs in minimising the oppressive costs of imported finished goods. There will always be some need for international trade as no country can be entirely self-sufficient in the modern age, but this should not be allowed to conceal the fact that much trade is only of benefit in bringing profit to traders. Prime examples of this are the air miles accumulated through trade in vegetables and fruit from distant locations that may have been better home-produced, for such transactions inflate prices for consumers as we have recently experienced in Britain. Furthermore, such policies make ridiculous the proper role of farmers, in turning them into so-called "guardians of the environment," whilst forbidding them the production of food.

The present danger of international corporate power bringing total financial collapse and chaos on a worldwide scale cannot be exaggerated. Much media publicity and some concern has recently been aroused through the increase of China's military empowerment in the Far East Pacific region, and calls have been made for the West to respond to this. It may be noted, however, that China is already in a position to conquer the world tomorrow without the need for firing a bullet. As leading American commentators have observed, it would only be necessary for China to call in her debts to bring the world to its knees in instigating a financial crash that would dwarf that of 1929, and again, would resound as a global catastrophe that none would escape. This is a conundrum that especially confronts American political thinkers at the present time: to promote protectionism or not, and if so, to what degree and how?

It is not due to the kindness of their hearts that the Chinese refrain from demanding what is rightfully theirs, but because she realises that such debts cannot possibly be repaid in the shorter term, and that the consequences of such a demand would rebound against her economy also. Nonetheless, the existing situation remains economically oppressive worldwide, and inevitably is slowly eroding the living standards and security of peoples throughout the advanced industrial economies. If, however, a major political crisis should occur through the "carelessness" of our leaders, China still retains the option to pull the plug in using financial catastrophe as a weapon that would be more long-term and destructive than any military alternative.

All the above arguments expose not merely the dangers but the existing harm currently inflicted by the present pattern of international finance, and so the fallacies of what is so nicely expressed as "Globalisation." Globalisation is still presented by the great hidden power wielders behind the throne of authority as the philanthropic economic solution for parties of both the left and right. Socialist and neo-liberals may perceive this ideology from different perspectives: the first, in lifting the poor of the world to a higher standard of living; and the second, as a successful mode in returning healthy profits to investors. If a differentiation is made between the supposed benefits of globalisation and the actuality of its outcome, a sharp contrast is revealed. Hence "Globalisation" is no more than a convenient propaganda term in misleading the gullible in different directions.

The essential need for promoting national interests is that democratic mechanisms can only be most effectively achieved through the nation state, and all other arguments follow from this. Although single issue questions may – and are effectively promoted through international organisations established for their purpose, the business of general government for the longer term has never been successful except when conducted within the nation state. That is, federations of one kind or another, or Continental empires comprising a mix of nationalities, have always encountered tensions, followed by struggles for independence, and eventually their breakup into separate parts.

The reason for this is that nation states, or separate peoples, most notably defined through language groups, have their own characteristics, traditions, and interpretations of similar or identical concepts – not to mention a variety of democratic systems in connecting the individual with ultimate authority. An effective two-way relationship between the individual and his representative or other direct contact authority, is irreplaceable for any working democracy, and up until the present time, this has not been practicable except within the framework of the nation state.

Following on from this, the takeover of the state or party political systems, by international financial power has clearly entailed a process of de-democratisation that has now reach intolerable proportions, and must be fought against in regaining independence. As we have argued at the start of this book, the formal establishment of democratic mechanisms, howsoever perfect they may appear in theory, is not sufficient in defining true democracy. One may either cite those examples of so-called democracies newly established in independent colonies from the early 1960s onwards, which almost immediately collapsed into tyrannical dictatorships; or those mature democracies in the advanced industrial economies in the 21st century, which were taken over in a serpentine fashion by the malign forces of Rentier capitalism. It should be noted, as John Dewey remarked, that democracy is "a culture and a set of practices, not merely a formal system."

A realistic strategy for the future of the advanced industrial economies calls for urgent discussion. One cannot simply turn a blind eye to future possible threats as if they did not exist. China is already by far the most powerful economy in the world, and although we should wish to continue our trade links with her, and further develop our friendship and cultural ties, that does not mean we should necessarily endorse everything that Xi Jinping has written in the recently published second volume of his massive book, *The Governance of China*, with its ideological call for Globalisation, and launched with the help of Prince Andrew, Duke of York, at the 2018 London Book Fair. And neither does it mean we should adopt America's possible attitude in loudly condemning China for her beliefs and practices, and overtly proclaiming the implementation of widespread import controls.

Instead, a middle course should be taken in identifying in turn, enterprise by enterprise and industry by industry, in gradually promoting manufactures through the latest technology and methods, whilst meanwhile discreetly introducing import duties and other controls. Such measures of import substitution should therefore not merely entail promoting the principle of self-sustainability, but the principle that every home-based product should be world competitive in terms of quality and commercial viability. Only through such a policy, in conjunction with exchange rate mechanisms, can international respect (as well as self-respect) in trading circles be retained whilst also imposing necessary import barriers. This is because the implementation of import controls when confined to protecting shoddy or indifferent products would expose a country to the contempt or ridicule of others for the pettiness of its narrow and insular attitudes. Hence dignity and self-respect are relevant values even in a commercial environment.

The following conditions should also be adhered to: import controls should only be applied to finished goods but not to raw materials. This is because the sole purpose of such controls should be confined to promoting import substitution, and not used as an excuse for countering unfavourable exchange rates that should be considered as falling into a separate department for government resolution.

In promoting the above policies, every country should encourage the development of national consciousness throughout every sector of the population, in safeguarding both cultural and economic integrity, in a world of international understanding and concord. National values are essential for cooperation and a desirable level of amiability, and the commercial success of any country may be measured against the extent of its national spirit.

It may also be noted that democracies exert a stronger and longer lasting underlying authority through the will of their majorities than any other form of government, and that full democracies exert a power that may be described as absolute. This is most vividly demonstrated through the almost universal repudiation by their peoples of collapsed dictatorships of any kind, and the joyful return of a democratic status of those nation states that had at one time been deprived of their freedom. The collapse of the East bloc, for example, revealed that supposedly invincible ideologies held with such conviction, had feet of clay, whilst the peoples of the three Baltic states recovered almost instantaneously the flourishing democratic regimes they had lost to tyranny fifty years earlier. This is not intended to demonstrate that democracy is necessarily in all circumstances the best form of government, but that amongst highly informed advanced industrial economies it is the most demanded.

If a better world is to emerge in the future, it is necessary that the advanced industrial economies concentrate on perfecting their own systems of government and society, rather than interfering or becoming involved in the troubles and conflicts of other nation states. This is because advanced industrial economies need to concentrate all their energy on their own good, if they are not to hinder progress or compromise their interests for a lesser cause. There is always the risk that in dissipating their energy elsewhere, they may become heavily engaged in the cost of foreign wars that empty their exchequers and demoralise their peoples with their hope for a better future.

This is not to suggest that regard for the wider world should be sacrificed for the cause of self-interest. On the contrary, it is suggested that the advanced industrial economies would be better placed to assist the wider world only after perfecting her systems of Full Democracy, for only then will her peoples have the confidence and will to pursue the unrestricted cause of all humankind for a philanthropic purpose.

Conversely, there is also the risk that foreign conflicts or other crises may unexpectedly drag the advanced economies into quarrels or situations that would have been better avoided had leaders been more percipient in anticipating consequences. In any event the future is always unknown, and unanticipated misadventures may always disrupt the path of civilisation and progress. And that is why the advanced industrial economies should at all times pursue their own best interests against all other distractions and external demands.

CHAPTER 6
The Recovery of Political Belief

"The Postmodernist and Postcolonialist claim that 'all
values are equally valid' is ... a major threat to democratic,
egalitarian values and individual liberty and, as such,
reveals itself to be just as devoid of moral and political
as of intellectual cogency."

Jonathan I. Israel, *Enlightenment Contested*, OUP, 2006,
p. 869.

As we have argued above, the first political concern of
any people should be promoting the interests of the
nation state, for history has demonstrated that it is the
only basis on which general government through democratic
mechanisms can operate successfully for the longer term. This
is because the two-way relationship in mediating between the
individual and state authority is dependent on so many cultural
and traditional factors that do not easily lend themselves to an
international interpretation.

But we live in a wider world of many and very different
nation states, and in such an international environment, for the
sake of harmony and friendly relationships amongst such
varied peoples, it is necessary to identify a set of principles to
which the informed worldwide majority may gladly adhere.
Such principles should be held with conviction across differing
cultures, and because of that factor and their intended appeal,
we have placed them under the heading of the Recovery of
Political Belief, as if lighting the lamp for a new
Enlightenment.

Such principles should not be concerned with the internal
governments of nation states, or attempts at interfering with the

socio-economic or cultural issues of their peoples, except through discreet diplomatic negotiations or informal voluntary exchange through cross-border groups; for each nation state should be respected for its unique identity, its status irrespective of size, or its stage of development if undergoing a process of rapid transformation. Such a Metternichian approach to international relations may be limited in its ambitions, but it is apt for stability and long-lasting peace, and unquestionably the only viable path in such a diverse world as we find today.

The recovery of political belief may be found by all peoples in all countries with good intent through the ideals and potential of our *Technological* civilisation. I use this term in preference to *Western* civilisation as there are nations in the Far East that have reached an equal technological status with that of the West – and indeed, may overtake the latter in the conceivable future. We are now entering an age when it would be audacious to use the term "Western" in referring to technological or social progress on a worldwide scale. This is not to suggest that no cultural differences exist between the two halves of the planet, but in the longer term it is technology that will decide the greatest changes of the future.

Whilst Japan is one of the leading democracies of the world, China falls into a different category. Although she aspires to promoting a democratic society in terms of equality of opportunity, raising the living standards of the majority, and assisting the unfortunate, she makes no pretensions to establishing democratic government based on the West European model. If the majority of her people are shortly to enjoy living standards equal or exceeding those experienced in Germany, France or Britain, her leaders may argue that this could not be achieved if the Western model of government is adopted, and hence that certain restrictions on freedom of expression may be justified to achieve this. Irrespective of the soundness of such an argument, it needs to be respected as that of an autonomous nation state.

However, any such untoward comparisons or comments stemming from the above remarks leave no room for smugness by the peoples of the West. As the earlier chapters of this book have shown, none of the major powers of Western Europe or the North American continent have yet achieved Full Democracy, whilst all are encumbered by serious problems. The fact that financial-industrial institutions have everywhere absorbed the power of parliamentary systems may have left in place the ghost of democratic mechanisms whilst destroying the reality of democratic government. Hence the question of democratic government is a worldwide issue, and not merely something to be pointed at here and there for a supercilious lecture on proper political conduct. We should never criticise others without being willing to acknowledge some degree of self-criticism.

If nation states choose not to establish a form of government that is offered or forced upon them, then for any reason they have a right to refuse. The great failing of America over the past 70 years has been her desperation in attempting to establish her own form of governance on peoples who either loathed the concept of democracy, or else were structurally and culturally quite unsuited to adopt such a form of government. There are many Islamic cultures in the Middle East, for example, that are antipathetic to democracy on religious or tribal grounds, or both, and would and are prepared to die in fighting against the idea for its promotion.

The pitiful striving of America, in her socio-historical ignorance of the outside world, to clumsily impose her distinctive form of democracy on developing territories has more often led to gruesome dictatorships and the loss of what remained of an earlier freedom. This is also intended as criticism of her appallingly negative view of the European imperial tradition in the immediate Post-War period, for although that tradition was far from perfect, it nonetheless held in place a semblance of order in difficult circumstances that were never properly grasped by the power across the water.

What all peoples, or at least majorities, are prepared to struggle for, are higher living standards and stability, howsoever these may be achieved. As democracy amongst certain territories is often seen as endangering stability, that is another reason amongst already unstable and backward regions to express antagonism towards this form of government. One of the better ways for increasing the living standards of a people, and ensuring much valued stability, is not to enforce an impractical system of government, but to restore or otherwise establish a constitutional monarchy. In this way, a sense of confidence is engendered in a head of state who is free of distracting vested interests and attains his position without bribery or corruption, and is then able to appoint ministers from the most competent, educated and respected members of the community.

Afghanistan, for example, has not experienced peace or security, since the fall of her monarchy in 1973, with the abdication of Zahir Shah who ruled from 1933, whilst his predecessor, the liberal, Amanullah Khan (1919-1929) strove courageously to raise his country to the standards of a Western democracy. Meanwhile, in Japan, it is unlikely that the country would have so successfully achieved its industrial pre-eminence in the Post-War period if it were not for the wisdom of the US General Douglas MacArthur in ensuring the ongoing status of Hirohito as emperor.

In further examining the question of constitutional monarchies, if the 16 West European states, prior to the collapse of the Soviet bloc, are listed as amongst the most advanced and democratic industrial economies in the world alongside America and Japan, then it is notable that 10 of these European states were constitutional monarchies; one of them being a Grand Duchy and two Principalities, in contrast to the 6 remaining republics. The value and predominance of constitutional monarchies amongst these leading democracies may in part be explained through the desirable influence of holding in check the self-importance and pomposity of elected representatives; ensuring a securer balance of power between legislative, executive and judicial authorities; and holding the majority population in awe and respect for the mystique of national power and identity. It may be questioned as to whether France – and especially Italy, would have experienced such unstable and chaotic administrations in the Post-War period if they had had the tranquil benefit of constitutional monarchs.

Britain, often cited as the leading European democracy, may trace her greatest development towards constitutional freedom, to the Dutch monarch William III, who was already experienced as the *Stadholder*, or chief magistrate, or kind of chairman, holding in place the diverse and difficult interests of the seven Provinces of the United Netherlands, when he ascended the throne. This monarch and his consort, Mary II, who ruled jointly, presented a European model for successful constitutional monarchy that has lasted until the present and through which may be traced every freedom enjoyed by the majority today.

Promoting technological civilisation is a cause which may appeal to all humankind, irrespective of culture or the material level of a people's development. However, although it may at once seize the imagination of the many, that is not to infer that all cultures have a positive mind-set towards developing its advance. There are cultures, well beyond the primitive stage, that are happy to embrace all the latest gadgets and mechanical aids, but are averse to a mind-set that encourages invention or innovation. The intense religiosity of the Saudis, for example, with their fixed ideas and static view of the world, denies them the curiosity to understand the new or the apparently inexplicable that they dismiss as things "not worth knowing." Such things are left in the mystery in which they exist. The Gulf Arab may, of course, change with the advance of time, or with the liberating emergence of a reforming prince, but then so will his values.

There is, therefore, a clear distinction between the users of modernity and those who create it. The initiators of modernity and invention are the great rule-breakers of humanity – the restless and discontented, ever in search of new solutions in overcoming the problems and conflicts of life. Their restless souls do not spring out of science and rationality, but rather from magic and spells in their defiance of the gods, in overcoming impossible odds. In their struggle for existence it is only with the alchemist in his vain striving to turn base metals into gold, or in the search for the elixir of life for eternal youth, that science first emerged as an accidental occurrence. If technological civilisation emerged through the striving for progress rather than the passive acceptance of change, then it has remained so until the present day. Likewise, an unconventional attitude, an insatiable curiosity, and a love of adventure is not only essential for technological progress, but for progress in every aspect of thought, exploration and imagination.

Technological civilisation is often frightening to the timid and hesitant for its infinite and unknown possibilities, for it challenges the fixed horizons of certainty, and seems to rival that only other sphere of infinity through the promises of religion. But such a fear should whither into insignificance if a modern interpretation is given to religion, and deistic truths are allowed to displace the older superstitions of a pre-scientific age. Hence it is the values of modern religion that call for change. All our material benefits: prosperity, medical science, long life, freedom from want and oppression, the joy of good health of those we cherish, are indebted to the benefits of technological civilisation. It may be that the will of God is expressed through the will of humankind, but it is only through the consciousness of the latter that good and progress is intentionally driven forward.

There is one aspect in which technological civilisation may be said to differ in its ethical purpose and prediction for the eventual fate of humankind by comparison with the long-held tradition of conventional religion. The Abrahamic religions foretell the eventual destruction of the world and all humankind in gloriously graphic detail, and the prediction is seized upon by fanatics and loudly proclaimed in the streets of cities throughout the Christian world. But such a belief is grossly immoral, irrespective of the original sources, and moreover, its teaching amounts to hardly less than a wicked mind-set.

This is not only because such a prediction cannot be factually substantiated, and that all pessimism tends to be malign, but more significantly, because such beliefs have a self-fulfilling element. It indicates an acknowledgement towards the act of self-immolation – even suicide, and a political situation may easily be conceived, when following a nuclear catastrophe, our leaders and great numbers of people might willingly accept the prediction as a falsely misleading religious comfort in the midst of destruction.

If one looks to Russia at the present day, and their troubles with the West, in conjunction with the intense religiosity of their Orthodox population, such an apocalyptic outcome is not difficult to imagine when a fatalistic pessimism may be turned on its head in fulfilling the "will" of an almighty deity. In turning to American civilisation in the recent past, they may equally be accused of a tendency towards this harmful Abrahamic line of thinking. During the Cold War their cry of "Better dead than Red," implies a passive acceptance of nuclear annihilation in place of a rational dialogue in settling difficult political differences. Such a slogan could only have emerged from a typical aspect of Christian fundamentalism as found across the Atlantic. In encouraging such scenarios of joyful immolation is clearly to be discerned the gross immorality of an aspect of traditional Biblical teaching.

Technological civilisation, on the other hand, does not present or encourage such pessimistic scenarios. This is because it is not obsessed with the sinfulness of humankind as something deserving the eventual extinction of our species. Its optimism is not driven by vain hopes or imaginary inventions, but by calls for practical steps in ensuring the eternity of the human race. The great High Priest of the future with a religious dimension should not be sought from amongst the leading clerics of our established churches, but rather from amongst our prominent scientists of the calibre of Stephen Hawking. When Hawking called for the need to occupy other planets in anticipation of an age when the earth might become uninhabitable, he was identifying practical measures for extending the survival of our species.

It may be that such attempts might end in failure, and that other scientists emerge with better solutions, but always the will is present for the betterment of humankind. Hawking, who loved the music-drama, would have known that when Siegfried broke Wotan's spear with *Nothung*, the trusty self-made sword, before ascending the fire-girt mountain to claim his sleeping bride, that that was the moment when man took over responsibility for his fate in usurping the power of the gods. An intelligent belief in the concrete should always be at the base of our philosophical outlook, rather than trust in unprovable abstractions that are lost in metaphysics.

As an international movement in unifying the peoples of the world, the cause of Technological civilisation should, for obvious reasons, be led by those already in its forefront. Thus, the prosperous countries of Western Europe, America, China, the Far East Tigers, and the Pacific dominions, should meet as equals in sharing secular values that give little or no rise to conflict. We have already indicated that it should not be the business of any nation state to interfere with the internal affairs of another, but there are important issues for humanity that can only be properly approached from an international perspective. Such issues promoting the universal welfare of humankind include, countering climate change, cleaning the environment, saving endangered species, capturing the waste disposal and elimination of plastics, attending to population control, and inter-planetary exploration.

The above inevitably entail cooperation calling for the introduction of internal policies within nation states, but such policies should only be in the cause of prioritising international needs and not intended to compromise or weaken state authority or threaten underlying cultural beliefs. Nonetheless, a clash of interests will on occasion inescapably occur, and that is why secular dominated states with their stronger leanings towards objectivity must succeed in somehow, through diplomacy or rational persuasion, in exerting their authority.

It is fortunate that the technologically most advanced nation states, as cited above, are collectively also the most powerful. As living standards and the stability of nation states may improve throughout the world, more countries may gradually be accepted into the fold of technological leadership. It may be noted that some large and even powerful states have been excluded from the above list, and several of those exclusions refer to countries that are experiencing uncertain times and the possibility of a troubled future. It is to be hoped that they attend successfully to their internal problems before joining the leading Technological bloc.

Whilst the most ambitious projects of technological civilisation, e.g., inter-planetary exploration, are unlikely to arouse resistance amongst the majority of world states, as their cost burden would be spread equally over the shoulders of wealthier peoples, there are other areas where resistance may be met, so calling for careful diplomacy.

Population control might be the most sensitive of these issues. It is also the most important question of all, since it is the root cause of all our environmental ills. Every question that is a threat to the environment is traceable to the pressures of population and unless we are aware of the fact that the erosion of the rainforests, the pollution of our rivers and lakes; the poisoning of arable land due to fertilisers; or the extinction of species due to hunting or fishing, etc., are the direct consequence of over-population, then humankind is destined to self-destruction. It may be true that the full consciousness of this only exists amongst the advanced economies of the world, and that the so-called Third world still lives in a state of innocence as to the threats ahead. And that is all the more reason for the advanced peoples to warn and enlighten their less-informed neighbours of the results of over-population as a moral imperative.

Although questions of population control were occasionally addressed by politicians and statesmen in the inter-War and Post-War periods until the start of the 1980s, since that time, there has been a mixture of confusion and silence in political circles, and the issue has only been raised in a non-political environment by such leading personalities in the scientific world as David Attenborough. Julian Huxley, the first Director-General of UNESCO, attempted to formulate a world population policy in the immediate Post-War period, whilst American advocates of population control within USAID (United States Agency for International Development) established a front organisation within that body, the United Fund for Population Activities which operated entirely outside the control of member nations. The issue was most alarmingly portrayed with the publication of Dr. Paul R. Ehrlich's book, *The Population Bomb*, in 1968, and shortly thereafter in 1972 appeared the Club of Rome's first report, *The Limits to Growth*, but following the election of President Reagan in 1980, with his cheery optimism and the rolling back of legislation, the neo-Malthusians reached the end of the road prior to their disappearance as a political influence.

The contrast between the advanced and developing peoples of our planet is illustrated by the fact that across the northern part of the globe birth rates are declining – even in China – and in Japan, disastrously so. A dramatic decline in birth rates is observable from locations as far distant as Vladivostock in the East to Reykjavik in the West, and Hammerfest in the north to Malta in the south – and Catholic populations are included no less than Protestant – and the North American continent must also be included in this list.

In all the above territories it is necessary to take serious steps in promoting population growth in safeguarding the cause of Technological civilisation. But another factor enters the matrix. Britain's overall population growth is now out of control, and is estimated to reach 75 million by 2050. Our roads and public transport system are already over-stretched to breaking point; whilst housing is desperately short, and there is resistance to building plans on agricultural land in many parts of the country; and although we have a generous rainfall, we are shortly to be threatened with severe water shortage in supplying essential needs. The above problems, however, all originate from mass immigration and the high birth rate of migrants. This introduces a difficult situation, for whilst the birth rate of the native population has collapsed and is declining further in instinctive response to the expansion of the world population, a threat is thereby presented to the cultural and economic integrity of the nation state. The issue is therefore raised as to the knotty question of differentiating between the native and migrant populations. Other countries in Europe are similarly affected by the same problems.

In the southern hemisphere, on the other hand, high birth rates are booming out of control, and for the most part, the problem should be attended to internally by each nation state, through the assistance of international negotiation. In such countries, it might be necessary to impose restrictions on foreign travel in the search for work, or in other words, to limit mass population movement from one territory to another.

The problem of deforestation is an issue that is equally urgent and just as difficult to resolve, and it is notable that both problems are currently ignored by politicians worldwide irrespective of the feelings of their peoples. The problems are also ignored by international institutions that are suitably placed to address such issues. Deforestation either occurs in the search for extending available farmland or else in the mining for minerals. As the jungles of Brazil, Central Africa, Indonesia and Papua New Guinea especially, act as the lung of the world, deforestation cannot be politically allowed to continue if humankind – and indeed, the entire animal kingdom is to survive. Again, deforestation is the consequence of over-population.

The first political line of defence of Technological civilisation is to save the primitive cultures of those who inhabit a jungle environment, and this may have a certain irony, but it does entail organising specific population sectors for desirable resistance. More effort will be needed in putting central government pressure on those promoting the extension of farmland and open mining, and if diplomacy fails to achieve its end in saving humankind from resulting extinction, then stronger measures would need the support of the world's wisest majority.

The cause of Technological civilisation, which also embraces the cause of the environment, as described above, is international in the sense that its attempt is ineffective or futile if reduced to a lesser level of authority. The constituent parts of the cause have been the subject of major single issue movements, but however large those movements have been, and despite their success on the public relations scale, they have never been sufficiently influential in actually exerting political power – nor could they have been. The same impotence applies to those nationally-based political parties that have sought to promote certain aspects of technological civilisation on a unilateral basis.

These seemingly impermeable problems indicate we do not live in an equal world, although we should like to believe the contrary, and furthermore, we assert that the world should by rights be more equal than it is, and to this end, we may even pretend it is so. But the reality is that nothing is equal, not amongst fauna where every living thing maintains its pecking order, and not amongst nations or peoples. The nearest we can defer to the idea of equality, is that all things are in a state of flux, that is, rising or falling within the margins of time, and in this is to be found the natural justice of the world when will and intelligence predominate in the longer term.

If this was not the outcome in the natural world, or in the domain of reason, then a Miltonic pandemonium would prevail where all and sundry would assemble to create uproar and chaos. In these truths are to be seen the weaknesses, intentional mischief, and calculated conflict emerging from our most significant (even if respected) international institutions that have failed us so often in the Post-War period, and if wisdom and stability in a peaceful environment is to flow from Technological civilisation, then a hierarchy of values needs to be respected.

Nation states at the present time may be divided into three differing categories: firstly, the advanced industrial economies, as already cited in this book; secondly, developing economies with aspirations towards joining with the above in promoting Technological civilisation; and thirdly, mischievous nation states that seek to disrupt harmony in many parts of the world in distracting the attention of their own populations from the internal ills of want and instability. It is not necessary to identify any of the states in either the second or third categories, as circumstances may quickly change that status at any time in bringing them into the greater fold, but it is necessary to recognise these disturbing factors in the cause of candid relationships as well as in the pursuit of harmony and success.

The central argument throughout this book is that the history of democracy in modern times has been an evolving process, and that when its summit has been reached with the attainment of Full Democracy, this will indicate the assumption of majority power as an actuality and no longer merely as an un-graspable ideal. From thenceforth, as noted in an earlier chapter, democracy will progress along a more predicable path of progress, until all peoples and nations stand together on a basis of equality in friendship and concord.

*

Guide to Further Reading

The following books not only set out to present a practical programme for the future, but more significantly, to create a new thinking or approach to political life for a just and upwardly aspiring egalitarian society. Perhaps more important still, they repudiate what has now become the self-destructiveness of the left/right divide. All the books cited below are addressed to the enquiring general reader, no less than to the academic or specialist –

Emergence of The New Majority, being Volume I of
Social Capitalism in Theory and Practice
ISBN 978-0-9556055-3-6   pp. xxxv/282   Royal Octavo
Notes, Appendices, Bibliography, Index

After analysing what should be the remit of political discussion in the *real* world, in differentiating between utopian and practical politics, the author describes the mismatch between the outdated mind-set of political parties and the transformation of society and the world of work over the past 60 years. This has increasingly led to the compounding rather than the resolution of major political problems. The breakdown of the old middle and working classes and their values is traced historically, and it is shown that this was brought about through changing patterns of employment, legislation towards a more egalitarian society, and other economic factors.

The emergence of the new middle-middle majority, with its different values, occurred whilst the political establishment was hardly aware of the fact. Although this new class is highly heterogeneous, at the same time, its specific but unheeded economic needs will eventually act as a catalyst for change. As a new class consciousness emerges through the realisation of these needs, the middle-middle majority will mutate into the all-powerful Responsible Society. The book concludes by addressing several current issues as an exercise in applying Social Capitalist principles.

The People's Capitalism, being Volume II of *Social Capitalism in Theory and Practice*
ISBN 978-0-9556055-4-3   pp. xx/461   Royal Octavo
Notes, Appendices, Bibliography, Index

This book begins by examining the nature of power in the contemporary world: in the world of politics, and more significantly, in the financial-industrial sectors which dominates the first. It examines how power is exerted in the Third world, and compares this with power in the advanced industrial economies. The limits of democracy and federations in upholding the interests of majorities is pointed out, and there is a call for radical changes to the economic system. Part II is concerned with socialising Productive capitalism and how this may be achieved politically. Part III entails an in-depth analysis of Rentier and Productive capitalism: how they operate internationally, and comparisons of their benefits and dis-benefits to society, and their differing macro-economic influences.

Part IV presents a pro-active strategy for the industrial trades unions in working to transform their employing enterprises from the Rentier to the Productive model. Part V on the Human Priorities of Politics delves into a number of philosophical and moral topics on society and government: e.g., on expediency versus justice; the self-justifying cynicism of vested interests; political realism in the just society; how to maximise the individual's potential; and, the desirable foundations for a disinterested politics. The book concludes with a description of the Responsible Society.

Prosperity in a Stable World, being Volume III of *Social Capitalism in Theory and Practice*
ISBN 978-0-9556055-5-0   pp. xx/473   Royal Octavo
Notes, Appendices, Bibliography, Indices

The book opens with 7 chapters on redefining the benefits of free trade in a world dominated by Productive capitalist economies. In such a world legislation would be in place to ensure that international trade was equitable and non-exploitative. There would be an end to usurious lending or investments, and instead, structures would be put in place for releasing the dead capital of the poor through extra-legal arrangements. The new practices of free trade would be linked into meeting the needs of the environment.

Part II is concerned with strategies for national prosperity, and describes the essential basics for a just economy in very simple terms. Such concepts as productivity, wealth creation, and ownership as a stewardship, are given precise definitions. Government policies for industry, and new modes for funding enterprises are covered in detail. Part III is concerned with job creation for Social Wealth. It begins by differentiating between Social and Unsocial Wealth Creation, and describes how industry and jobs have been undermined by Rentier capitalistic practices. Towards correcting the imbalance between public and private sectors, occupational priorities are listed according to productivity; the invisible barriers to trade are identified; and proposals are put forward for reversing manufacturing decline, together with special legislation in increasing the profitability of the productive sector.

Part IV on reforming the business enterprise is concerned with the nature of the Company: identifying its intrinsic purpose; fairness and efficiency as one; and a proposed General Purposes clause for the company. There is also a chapter which discusses the different concepts of usury and as to their relevance today. Part V: Forty-Three Failing Britain, an exercise in the critique of Rentier capitalism, is an attack on a powerful group of corporate directors following their letter published in *The Times* shortly before a general election. Part VI concludes the book with a 49-page Declaration of Social Capitalist Values.

Egalitarianism of The Free Society *and the end of class conflict*
ISBN 978-0-9556055-2-9   pp. xviii/317   Royal Octavo
Notes, Bibliography, Index

This book is an adjunct to *Social Capitalism in Theory and Practice*, in that it expands on several subordinate yet important themes raised in the 3-volume work. Part I comprises 6 chapters on the relationship between Culture and Egalitarianism. Then follow 11 chapters on the Politics of Property which examine the psychological nature of possession, and in pursuing the argument of one of the greatest 19th century philosophers, the author demonstrates that the individual can only reach his full potential through the ownership and use of property.

Property is then described in the different forms in which it occurs in society, including communal and collective property. Part III, Democracy: Real and Illusory, begins by outlining the erosion of freedom in the contemporary world, followed by a clear differentiation between the democratic way of life and democratic government, and how the one may exist without the other. For example, whilst India purports to have a democratic government, its society is severely wanting in democratic values. Singapore, on the other hand, has an ideally democratic and multi-racial society, but its government tends towards authoritarianism. Several commonly held beliefs about British democracy are exploded, and there is a discussion as to when the benefits of democracy are maximised.

The book concludes with 12 chapters on the Road to Constructive Politics, being a critique of 20th century epistemological theories and practices, acting as a barrier to constructive thought. In the revolt against reason, philosophical pragmatism is targeted for particular criticism. The nature of reason is examined, and the reality of ideas is upheld as an essential tool for the intelligent discussion of the material world. The book concludes with an appeal for establishing a New Idealism, the proponents of which would use a methodology very different from their predecessors.

The Future of Politics *with the demise of the left/right confrontational system*
ISBN 978-1-906791-46-9   pp. xvi/188   Demy 8vo
Notes, Index

The left/right confrontational system is coming to an end, since it is failing to further promote the interests of majorities worldwide. For 200 years it has acted as the linchpin of democracy, and politics is almost unthinkable without referring to the concepts of the Left or the Right.

This book describes how the old confrontational system has fulfilled a vital function for the progress of humanity, but how in advanced industrial economies everywhere, it is now reaching the end of its useful purpose. This is not only reflected in the collapse of party memberships globally, but in the tendency of legislation and the executive to compound rather than resolve the issues of our age.

Meanwhile, a new class is emerging in the advanced industrial world, which the author describes as the middle-middle 90%+ majority. Because contemporary parties are trapped in a time-warp of the past, they are unable to represent the interests of this new majority.

The most urgent political issue of our time – heightened by the debt-fuelled financial crisis – is the need to make the banking and corporate sectors socially responsible. This book outlines a practical strategy towards this end. Only when that is achieved will it be possible to address effectively such pressing issues as climate change.

Over the past 60 years society and the world of work have been transformed out of all recognition. Whilst the world of actuality has raced ahead, political thought has lagged behind – unable to keep apace with the significance of real events.

In the light of this situation, the author points to the necessity for a fresh approach to political thought in breaking the existing mould. New and more effective democratic mechanisms are needed to ensure a socially just and equitable society for a better future. Hence the now malign left/right concepts of the past must be repudiated forever.

The Democratic Imperative *the reality of Power Relationships in the Nation State*
ISBN 978-1-909421-14-1   pp. viii/234   Royal Octavo
Notes, Index

Democracy understood as people power, which is the only proper definition of the word, is put forward in this book as the panacea for resolving the most pressing issues of our time. But democracy as a practicable system hinges on many conditions which are seldom appreciated by our world leaders, international institutions, or relevant bodies of learning.

The evolution of democracy as a system of government and way of life, and the problems to which the former gives rise is broadly discussed by the author. Of most significance are those situations, in both East and West, when democracy is ideologically used as a cover for ulterior purposes.

It is powerfully argued that the left/right divide which for 200 years has served as the rationale for advancing social progress in sustaining democracy is now *destroying* it, as partly witnessed through the collapse of both party memberships and voting figures in most advanced industrial economies. This has occurred through the transformation of society and the world of work over the past 60 years, and has left our parliamentary representatives trapped in a time-warp of the past in their inability to meet the actuality of contemporary issues.

It is clearly shown, through a variety of reasons, that democracy as an all-inclusive system of government is only workable within the nation state. This partly explains the crises of the EU, and the shortcomings of the UN's Security Council. The greatest threat to democracy, since it limits the power of the nation state to carry through electoral promises, is international finance and transnational corporations, which are unaccountable to any responsible authority and liable to bring economic catastrophe in their wake.

This is a book which seeks to empower our national politicians, irrespective of party, so they may more effectively represent the interests of their electorates. A way must be found for our politicians to resolve their predicament, even though it may entail a shift in their attitudes and ideals.

The Death of Socialism *the irrelevance of the traditional left and the call for a progressive politics of universal humanity*
ISBN 978-1-906791-14-2   pp. xvi/174   Demy 8vo
Notes, Index

The author wrote this book after 14 years as an activist, both locally and nationally as a Labour party member. He describes his efforts to update the thinking and attitudes of the party to fit the needs of today's contemporary majority. With this in mind, he attempted to establish a New Socialism, which would not only be more objective in outlook but eschew class-based prejudices. The purpose of politics in the 21st century, surely, was not to nurture old resentments or fight old battles, but to resolve substantive issues in creating a just and egalitarian society.

Although Labour party members today rarely openly promote the idea of class struggle, the author discerned a deeply-felt psychological attitude which was more concerned with "knocking" the opposition than resolving difficult issues for the benefit of all society. Worse still, the attitudes and actions of the Labour party and socialism betray they are not fighting for a classless all-inclusive society, but rather for a proletarian society modelled after their own ideals in discriminating against the rest of the population. The final chapters of the book argue it is necessary to transcend the self-destructive conflicts of the past, through practical politics ensuring an all-inclusive society for justice and equity for all.

Populism Against Progress *and the collapse of aspirational values*
ISBN 978-0-9543161-8-1   pp. xviii/152   Demy 8vo
Notes, Index

This book opens with a description of the hidden poison of populism which is not only undermining democracy but threatens to destroy Western civilisation. In the second chapter this is contrasted with the beneficent power of culture with its channels for creativity on one hand, and bonding mechanisms for understanding and communication on the other. There then follow chapters on the populism of Islamic fundamentalism and how this is hindering the progress of their own people; the battle for freedom through education; social bonding through cultural education; and how populism is adversely affecting the achievement of an upwardly aspiring egalitarian society.

This leads to considering the self-destructiveness of contemporary politics, followed by chapters on corporate power and the corruption of society, and the debasement of culture through marketing strategies. The book concludes with a consideration of those philosophical and educational influences which may be called upon to combat populism and promote higher aspirational values.

Deism and Social Ethics *the role of religion in the third millennium*
ISBN 978-0-9543161-9-8   pp. xx/201   Demy 8vo
Notes, Appendix, Bibliography, Index

Following a period earlier in the 20th century when it was assumed that secularism had finally come to dominate political life worldwide, in the 21st century we now find ourselves living in a very different environment. The influence of religion in political life is now becoming increasingly significant in many parts of the world. In those areas where majorities are more intellectually developed, i.e., in Western Europe and the Confucian countries of the Far East, secularism remains firm in politically guiding the future.

Two questions are raised in this book: firstly, it has now been physiologically demonstrated that the religious temperament is an essential part of the human psyche (although differing in intensity from one person to another) and hence it is ineradicable. The issue in the modern world, therefore, arises as to the desirability of religion without superstition or revelation. The second question arises as how best to communicate with those regimes dominated by religion when the latter is the only basis for personal trust. The author argues for integrity and truth in considering religious questions, as otherwise insincerity and falsehood may lead to mistrust and the failure of political negotiations in the international sphere.

The book presents the need for the deistic beliefs of the early 18th century, but updated with regard to defining the nature of the deity. It promotes a form of deism, based on reason and philosophical principles, enabling a first step on the ladder of religion without commitment to myth, superstition or theology.

Deism as an approach to religion would therefore ideally fulfil the healthy sceptical needs and love of freedom, of enlightened humankind in the third millennium. Meanwhile, in the realm of diplomacy, in acknowledging with conviction the existence of God, it would help bring different faiths towards a common political purpose. The book also presents a critical review and appreciation of leading faiths throughout the world.

Freedom From America *for safeguarding democracy and the*
economic and cultural integrity of peoples
ISBN 978-0-9543161-5-0   pp. xviii/222   Demy 8vo
Notes, Appendices, Index
   Also available in Arabic, published by Dar-Al-Salam in Cairo
<u>www.dar-alsalam.com</u>

The book opens with the contention that "the American mind-set is distinct from that of any other people or race on earth in a way that no other peoples or races are distinct from one another." Whilst acknowledging that America has produced valued bodies of specialised learning and research, and assenting with G.K. Chesterton's quip, that "the real American is all right; it is only the ideal American who is all wrong," the author then begins to analyse these false values which have made the American character. These stem from a particular type of materialism, whereby money and its acquisition is put on a pedestal above human and other values. This has led inevitably not only to an extreme form of greed, but to deceit and the disguising of motives and attitudes in the service of material gain. These unpleasant characteristics are in turn covered up by a false amiability and superficiality in human relationships.

Out of such a society has developed a highly sophisticated Rentier capitalistic system offering a wide range of usurious financial products. The opening chapter describes an international situation whereby America finds herself versus the rest of the world, in terms of corporate power, and a political ideology convinced it has a God-given mission to culturally absorb all peoples throughout the planet. Chapter 2 is concerned with America and the Deception of the World; Chapter 3 is entitled America and the Debasement of Cultural

Values; and Chapter 4, America and the Debasement of Democratic Values, through the emergence of the plutocratic state.

The last two chapters discuss ways in which the world may be liberated from American hegemony. Chapter 5 is entitled, A Global Strategy for the Planet and Humankind, in considering environmental issues in addition to an enlightened business culture, and the need to confront America as an ethical imperative. The last chapter, De-Fusing the Causes of Terror, investigates the injustice and anarchy in many parts of the world stemming directly from American intervention, either direct or covert through such agencies as the CIA. World terrorism can never be defeated through the American war machine – although it may be worsened. It can only be defeated through enabling justice and granting national rights to oppressed peoples.

Our Swindling Finance Houses *their exploitation of the vulnerable*
ISBN 978-0-9538460-5-4   pp. xxi/121   Demy 8vo

Using the pseudonym of Guy Tallice, the author describes his horrific 6-month stint in working for a major finance services company, and household name, at the end of the 1980s. Having been made redundant as a senior executive of a manufacturing enterprise, and desperate to find work to keep up mortgage payments, and maintain a family with 3 young children, he joined Allied Dunbar as a Sales Associate.

The book opens with a Preface sub-headed Swindling Within The Law, which examines in some detail different modes of fraud and sleight of hand used to confuse or deceive the public. He shows how financial services use swindling methods throughout the industry, and concludes with an appeal for legislation to define and make swindling an illegal activity. He then vividly describes the guile of recruitment methods, and the ingenuity of deceit in inveigling the unemployed into their organisation.

During the Thatcherite era when industries were going bust and unemployment was soaring, there were only Phony Jobs in A Phony World, being the title of the opening chapter. The second chapter, Ripe for Exploitation, describes in detail the pain of unemployment together with its adverse psychological effect on the personality, and the stress it brings to family life. The third chapter, What Dreams are Made of, describes the recruiting procedures, with promises of riches for those working for the company. The fourth chapter, The Glory Days, outlines the author's working experience and early success.

Using hard-selling methods, after an intensive training course, he approached every relative, friend, neighbour, and casual acquaintance, to buy Personal Pension plans. In addition, he approached industrial enterprises, and in one factory sold personal pension plans to a number of semi-literate manual workers on the minimum legal wage. Back at the office he was held up by the branch manager as an example of the ideal Sales Associate. The author, however, could meanwhile not understand the downcast attitude and apparent apathy of colleagues – or not until it was too late.

The subsequent chapters expose the huge swindle inflicted on Sales Associates, each of whom supposedly had a separate and secret arrangement with his manager on the mode of remuneration. The author called a meeting of his colleagues and they cooperated in a rescue plan for disengagement from the company, meeting secretly in the office late in the evening, and using available facilities in photocopying CVs in an attempt to find real jobs. Although the author was never paid the commission he had earned, and incurred heavy debts by the time he left the company, he escaped lightly by comparison with several colleagues who lost their homes and personal assets, due to extortionate loans forced on them by managers to maintain business and living costs.

When the swindle was finally uncovered, the author turned on his colleagues, asking why they had not warned him of the fraud into which they had all fallen. Their simple answer was: "But we all had our different arrangements and we didn't know what yours were. When the mask was taken off we just felt stupid. Now don't you feel the same?" – "No," replied the author, "I just feel swindled." Drawing together all the facts, he wrote to Sir Mark Weinberg, Chairman of the company who had been knighted the previous year at the instigation of Margaret Thatcher for developing the financial services industry. The letter was copied to several other directors. The letters went unacknowledged, but the matter was passed to senior managers who called a meeting to talk through the problem, but despite flattering gestures, discussions ended in futile circular arguments.

The author's career with Allied Dunbar was brought to a sudden halt following serious injuries during a crash as a front seat car passenger, after signing up a major contract with an engineering company, together with a senior colleague, as they sped away at high speed in elated spirits, realising they would shortly be £4,000 richer. After 3 years litigation, the author was persuaded (through the burden of debts) to accept a derisory compensation payment from the company for his injuries. Shortly after hospitalisation, the author visited his remaining colleagues in their office to be cheerfully met with the revelation that Allied Dunbar had arranged for them to receive Social Security benefits. And these were the employees of one of the wealthiest financial services institutions in the UK!

The final chapter proposes reforms in cleaning up the industry. In the first print run of the book there was, absurdly, a Dedicatory Petition to the Labour Government elected into power on 7th June 2001, to "initiate legislation to curb the greed dishonesty and scams of the financial institutions." It was not fully realised at the time that the Labour government would promote the interests to the usurious economy to Thatcherite proportions.

Land of The Olympians *papers from the enlightened Far North*
ISBN 978-1-906791-17-7   pp. 264   Royal Octavo
Notes, Index

This book reprints articles originally published in the 1960s in the Finnish press and learned journals, during the author's 10-year residence in Scandinavia. The leading series of 8 articles, *How To Be An Olympian*, were published in the country's leading intellectual journal, and comprise a study of neutrality in Sweden and Finland and how it affected social and political attitudes. The author praises the cool objectivity and sagacity of neutral Scandinavians in their socio-political outlook, comparing this favourably with the stressful, excitable, and often prejudicial environment of those countries unhappily caught up in the Russo-American conflict.

Here was a haven of peace, security, and sanity, in a world which was otherwise constantly in fear of nuclear war. The author raises the question of Britain and Continental Europe forming into a neutral but militarily powerful bloc, possibly at the instigation of Gaullist France, as a defence against the ideological fanaticism of Russo-America. Two other series of articles, published in Finland's second largest daily, comprise studies of the entrenched English class system, comparing it with the egalitarian and democratic societies of Scandinavia, with their higher living standards and greater freedom.

Other articles (several of which were illustrated with cartoons) take a wryly humorous look at Finnish life; and then there is a short story, *What The Watchdog Saw*, being a savage satire on the skulduggery of both the left and right in the Britain of the 1960s. The book concludes with a lecture, *Internationalism and Europe*, originally delivered in 1964, in which the author argues that Europe is ideally placed, through her greater maturity, to take realistic measures for establishing a more peaceful world in intervening between the abrasive political extremism of two larger powers.

The Social Capitalist Network
www.socialcapitalistnetwork.org

INDEX

Lightning Source UK Ltd.
Milton Keynes UK
UKHW01f1146260818
327819UK00001B/12/P